ASPECTS OF LEEDS 2

ASPECTS *of* LEEDS 2
Discovering Local History

Edited by
Lynne Stevenson Tate

Series Editor
Brian Elliott

Wharncliffe Publishing

First Published in 1999 by
Wharncliffe Publishing
an imprint of
Pen and Sword Books Limited,
47 Church Street, Barnsley,
South Yorkshire. S70 2AS

Copyright © Wharncliffe Publishing 1999

*For up-to-date information on other titles produced under the
Wharncliffe imprint, please telephone or write to:*

> **Wharncliffe Publishing**
> **FREEPOST**
> **47 Church Street**
> **Barnsley**
> **South Yorkshire S70 2BR**
> **Telephone (24 hours): 01226 - 734555**

ISBN: 1-871647-59-2

A CIP catalogue record of this book is available from the
British Library

Cover illustration: City Square 1903 used by kind permission of the Leeds Civic Trust.

Printed in Great Britain by
Redwood Books, Trowbridge, Wiltshire

CONTENTS

INTRODUCTION

by Lynne Stevenson Tate

THE LAUNCH OF *ASPECTS OF LEEDS 1* IN 1998 was something of a landmark for Wharncliffe Books, as it was the first of the series to be located outside of South Yorkshire where *Aspects of Barnsley* and *Aspects of Rotherham* had been set with some success. Since that time other titles in the *Aspects* series have begun to appear at regular intervals and, by the year 2000 the series will cover much of the country. The reason behind this rapid expansion of the list is that each book offers a mix of well-researched, academic historical studies with the more informal 'nostalgic' nature of articles which are based on family history and reminiscences. Within each *Aspect* title there should be something to appeal to most readers and this latest volume, *Aspects of Leeds 2*, offers as many diverse articles as did *Aspects of Leeds 1*.

The City of Leeds is, in the minds of many people, inextricably linked with it's football team. Even those who are not keen followers of the game of football, or were not even born then, know all about what has been termed 'the Glory Years' of Leeds United, under the managership of Don Revie. David Saffer and Howard Dapin take us back to the 'breakthrough' season of 1964-5 when, led by their captain, Bobby Collins, Leeds United narrowly missed bringing the FA Cup to Leeds for the first time. In the first volume of *Aspects of Leeds* Robert Preedy took the reader on a trip back in time with his article of Leeds cinemas. During his researches into this article Robert became aware that Leeds had it's own 'mover and shaker' in the cinema world with one Claude H Whincup. In his article Robert shows how, while holding a number of positions within the Cinema Exhibitors Association, Claude Whincup helped steer his association through the minefield of post-war legislation and the advent of wide-spread television.

Aspects of Leeds 2 covers a wider geographical area of the city than the first volume. Rothwell has been famous for many years because of it's whale jaw bones and William Banks relates their chequered history and near loss. Kathleen Gurney's article deals with New Leeds, which is the area now known as Sheepscar and Chapeltown. Kathleen's parents and grandparents lived for many years in this area of Leeds and her article interweaves the actual history of the area with her own family history and personal memories.

Hunslet is an area of Leeds long associated with industry of all kinds. This was especially true in the nineteenth and early twentieth centuries, but John Goodchild shows how the seeds of the industrialisation of this area were actually sown a century or so earlier when entrepreneurs such as Abraham Fenton and Charles Brandling opened collieries in the Hunslet area. The Aire and Calder Navigation had reached Leeds Bridge by 1700 and consequently the river Humber and the ports of Hull and Goole were now within easier reach for the manufacturers and coal barons. The negotiations concerning the construction of Middleton Colliery's wooden waggonway took years to complete and not only went to the Sheriff's Court but also to Parliament in 1758 when a special Act of Parliament for 'establishing Agreements' was sought. As in many other areas where a ready supply of coal was to be found, other industries soon established themselves and Hunslet quickly became one of the main sites of industry within the environs of Leeds. Ray Dobson was born and brought up in that other area of Leeds where the sighting of heavy industry was dependent on cheap, quick transport, and that was Holbeck with its network of railway lines. Ray's piece reflects on family life during the 1930s, arguably the most difficult of times in this century. For me, the importance of the role that the Co-op and it's 'divvy' or dividend played in many families lives is highlighted here, and I wonder how many readers of this article will find that they are able to remember either their own, or their parents Co-op number?

The name Quarry Hill has resonance for many a 'Loiner' who can remember the dominating presence of that great 1930s experiment in municipal housing at the bottom of Eastgate. Jane Greenwood unearths a rich history of the area from earliest times right up to the present day and in the process introduces us to the famous and the more infamous residents of this area of Leeds. These have included murderers, famous actresses and radical social reformers. Large areas of back-to-back housing were built by early, terminating, building societies as a speculative venture. The houses were built to a plan and were to provide rented accommodation for the rapidly emerging artisan class. Throughout the eighteenth century however, the area deteriorated and became highly insanitary and was visited by periodic outbreaks of cholera and later typhus. By 1882 the condition of the East End of Leeds had become a public scandal but still the area continued to attract the growing immigrant Irish and Jewish communities. The development of Quarry Hill Flats was an early effort in slum clearance; a policy carried out more thoroughly in the 1960s.

Being born in Bradford and brought up in Pudsey, a trip to Leeds was for me as a child, something of a treat and as my grandfather worked on the railways we always went to Leeds on the train. My first memory of Leeds is walking out of the concourse of Leeds City station and seeing what appeared to be a huge roundabout which had a large statue of a man mounted on a horse. I was later told that this was a statue of the Black Prince. That set of a number of follow up questions from me such as *'Why the Black Prince?'* and *'When did he come to Leeds?'* to which my poor harassed father replied as many other parents have done before and since *'I don't know!'* So I was delighted to receive William Scott's article on City Square and the Black Prince. Finally the answer to my original query? Well, read the article and find out for yourself!

Both Anthony Silson and Maureen Thorp address the subject of education in their articles. Anthony's article is concerned with Bramley and the central role that the churches and chapels took on in the social growth of the village. Predominant in all of their ventures was the spread of educational opportunity for the children of the village but this was also supported by the strong ethos of 'self-help' and 'self-improvement' that were so much a part of life during the Victorian years. Maureen attended St Anne's School in Woodhouse Square for a time during the early 1950s. This was a Catholic School, run and staffed primarily by nuns from one of the Catholic church's teaching orders, with a small number of lay staff. This was a mixed school, only to the extent that boys and girls attended the school, but for all lessons, boys and girls were taught separately. The year Maureen has chosen to write about was the Coronation year of 1952-3, and the article is so evocative of a time long past as, after Vatican II, much was altered within Catholic schools with regard to the teaching methods and the syllabus. The excitement for many children of the Coronation year is recalled by the recollection of the Children's Day celebrations that year and the school outing.

The final two articles are concerned with industry. The clothing and tailoring industry has always been an important part of the Leeds industrial scene and especially of the Jewish history of Leeds. Zimmerman's was a tailoring firm that had been founded by a Lithuanian Jewish immigrant in the late 1880s. It was a proud boast of the Zimmerman's that they had supplied clothing for the first Burton's shops in the early years of the twentieth century. Isadore

Pear went to work in the family clothing factory in the years prior to the Second World War and has given us a fascinating insight into the working practices of the clothing trade at this time and how the family business truly was the family business. The last article by William Scott is a fascinating account of an industrial strike that occurred during the winter of 1891-2, by the employees of the Aire and Calder Navigation company. William Scott has spent many years researching the history of the Aire and Calder Navigation company and came across the company's record of the dispute. He has produced a fascinating and chilling account of the progress of the strike, from onset to settlement in which the key players were not only local people but national figures such as Ben Tillotson who appeared for the Union. Tillotson had made his name in the many London Docks disputes and eventually became a Labour MP.

On behalf of the authors and myself, may I take this opportunity to thank all of those librarians, archivists, curators and support people who have enabled these articles to have been written. My thanks a particularly due to Charles Wickert of the Civic Society who searched for some of the the photographs in the book and Dr Kevin Grady and the Civic Society for permission to reproduce these. I would also like to express my gratitude to the family of William Banks for allowing me to continue with the publishing of his article after his death on 26 December 1998. I wish I had met him in person.

Thanks are due, as always, to the team at Wharncliffe: Brian Elliott, the series editor, Charles Hewitt, the Chief Executive, Barbara Bramall, Production Manager and Paul Wilkinson, Designer. I would like to thank Mike Parsons, the Imprint Manager, whose patience, persistence and perseverance during a particularly difficult year for me, has proved invaluable.

At home it would be impossible for me to function properly without the continuing support and encouragement of my husband Michael, so I here register my thanks to my chief bottle-washer, coffee maker and dedicated message taker.

Lastly I would like to dedicate this book to the memory of my parents Peter and Jean Stevenson. They were always incredibly supportive of all I ever did, but sadly, they never lived to see me 'in print'.

1. LEEDS UNITED: THE BREAKTHROUGH SEASON 1964 -1965

by David Saffer and Howard Dapin

WHILST FOOTBALL IS ONLY A GAME, and Leeds United only a football team, if you find yourself in conversation with someone not from this island who has heard of our city, it is almost certain that their knowledge was gained from our teams' exploits on the field.

Looking back at their history Leeds United have won three League Championships, one FA Cup, one League Cup, and two major European trophies. Between 1968 and 1974 they were regarded by many as the greatest club side in European football. However, they did not always have this status.

Leeds United were founded in 1920, rising phoenix-like out of the charred remains of Leeds City who were unceremoniously thrown out of the football league for ineligible payments to players. Prior to Revie's appointment, Leeds had won a Second Division title and been promoted a further three times from Division Two. In addition, despite having had some great players representing them, notably the legendary John Charles, the team had existed in a twilight zone between the top two divisions, playing in the main mediocre football which failed to set the football world alight.

Supporters had not had too much to cheer about; this was about to change. When we examine where their success began it was arguably the day Harry Reynolds, then chairman, appointed Don Revie as player-manager in March 1961:

Although Don had no experience of management he had a wealth of football knowledge. Don was interested in the player-manager's job at Bournemouth. I gave him permission to apply. When I was writing his reference it occurred to me that with all these recommendations we could do with him ourselves. So I tore up the letter and offered him the Leeds job.[1]

For Revie it was his chance, and he knew it:

I'd been thinking about the chance of a manager's job for some time and kept wondering which club might be the right one for me. This one suited me down to the ground. I knew something had to be done,

Figure 1. The Leeds United squad that embarked on the 1964/5 campaign. *Back Row* (L-R): Bell, Reaney, Goodwin, Sprake, Williamson, Hunter, Lawson. *Front Row* (L-R): Giles, Bremner, Storrie, Collins (Captain), Revie (Manager), Weston, Greenhoff, Charlton. The trophies are the West Riding Cup and Football League Second Division Championship Trophy. *Photograph used courtesy of Yorkshire Evening Post Newspapers*

so I thought we would improve the image with a new strip, especially an all-white one like Real Madrid's. That gave me the chance to tell them that I wasn't going to be satisfied until we had reached the same stature as the famous Spanish club. There was no future at Leeds for anybody who did not think that way. [2]

Revie quickly set about blending youngsters like Billy Bremner, Norman Hunter, and Paul Reaney, with intelligent purchases from other clubs, in particular Bobby Collins from Everton. Revie knew what he was looking for with Collins:

He is the perfect example of what we in the game call a professional's professional. Bobby's aim was always to do things simply and quickly. He never tried to be too clever on the ball for the sake of his own glory. I have never come across anyone with such a fierce will-to-win and dedication to the game. These qualities immediately rubbed off on the players around him at Elland Road, from the juniors to the first teamer's. Bobby regarded it as a personal insult to be beaten. I had been searching for some time for a midfield 'general' with the character and skill to really motivate the team, and Bobby fitted the bill perfectly. [3]

After just avoiding relegation to the Third Division on the last day of the 1961/62 season, United consolidated in 1962/63 finishing a creditable fifth. Revie and his team were now ready. With the addition of Johnny Giles, signed from Manchester United, clinched the 1963/64 Second Division title in the last game at Charlton Athletic. Leeds arrived in the top league determined to prove they were there to stay (Figure 1).

Prior to the start of the season Revie's Leeds were labelled as the hardest and most uncompromising team in the football league by an official FA report that analysed 'bookable' offences. This was slightly misleading because the majority of cautions were awarded in junior matches, not first team football. Unfortunately the damage was done; Leeds had acquired a reputation.

Undaunted, Leeds set about making their mark and the 1964/65 season proved to be 'the breakthrough' for the club. Leeds started the campaign in storming fashion winning their first three games; more solid performances pushed them to the higher echelons of the table. There were many bruising encounters, none more than the league clash with Everton at Goodison Park where Leeds emerged with a one-goal victory. The score however was overshadowed by unsavoury scenes which saw not only an Everton player sent off, but also both sets of players being led from the pitch by the referee to calm down.

Throughout the season Leeds stayed near the top challenging Manchester United. In the end a crucial Easter defeat against their arch-rivals was to prove decisive. Leeds were never to recover the top spot and lost out in the championship race on goal difference.

Photograph by courtesy of the "Yorkshire Evening Post"

versus

Southport   № 5161

F.A. CUP 3rd ROUND
SATURDAY, 9th JANUARY, 1965.

OFFICIAL PROGRAMME 6d

Though heartbreaking it had truly been a wonderful effort by the young pretenders.

If the league campaign had been momentous, then the FA Cup run really caught the supporter's imagination, and if anything placed the team even more in the public eye. Before the 1964/65 competition each season in the FA Cup for Leeds United had ultimately ended in disappointment. Indeed, Leeds had only previously reached the last eight once, in 1949/50, when Major Buckley's team lost to Arsenal 1-0 at Highbury.[4] This year however they were playing so powerfully that the bookmakers regarded them as one of the pre-tournament favourites for the first time ever.

Third Round   9 January 1965

Leeds United   3 (1)   Greenhoff (20), Johanesson (81), Johnson (84)
Southport   0 (0)

Attendance: 31,927
Receipts: £9,008
Referee: Mr G Grundy (Grimsby)

Leeds United: Sprake, Reaney, Cooper, Bremner, Charlton, Hunter, Greenhoff, Storrie, Johnson, Collins, Johanesson
Southport: Harris, Cunningham, Cairns K, Peat, Darvell, Beanland, Dagger, Cairns R, Davies, Russell, Spence

Leeds were given the comfort of a home draw against Fourth Division Southport at the start of their forty-fifth FA Cup campaign.

Figure 2. Leeds played before capacity crowds from the fourth round, supporters soon became used to long queues for tickets. This scene outside the ticket office would become common place during the 'Revie' years.

Photograph used courtesy of Yorkshire Evening Post Newspapers

As expected they disposed of their brave opponents, but not without one or two scares. After twenty minutes of gentle sparring Leeds first goal arrived; Greenhoff scoring with a cracking left foot cross-shot from eighteen yards. However, if their fans expected the floodgates to open they were to be sadly disillusioned.

Southport, showing tremendous determination throughout, played some neat football but failed to produce any clear openings. They also enjoyed more than their fair share of good fortune as United struck the woodwork four times. Only when they seemed to tire visibly in the last ten minutes were Leeds able to extend their lead. On eighty-one minutes Storrie set Reaney free down the right flank, his cross found Johanesson who prodded the ball home. Soon it was 3-0 when Johnson touched in Cooper's fine cross. The score flattered Leeds and they knew that to progress further in the competition they would have to improve.

Fourth Round 30 January 1965

Leeds United 1 (0)   Storrie (58)
Everton 1 (0)   Pickering (pen 66)

Attendance: 50,051
Receipts: £13,000
Referee: Mr K Howley (Billingham-on-Tees)

Leeds United: Sprake, Reaney, Bell, Bremner, Charlton, Hunter, Giles, Weston, Storrie, Collins, Johanesson
Everton: West, Wright, Wilson, Gabriel, Labone, Stevens, Scott, Harvey, Pickering, Temple, Morrissey

These two teams met in the same round the previous season. Leeds were determined to prevent a repetition of the result, and supporters were desperate not to miss the encounter (Figure 2). 50,000 fans crammed into Elland Road expecting a ferocious tie, especially after the torrid affair at Everton earlier in the season. The hostile atmosphere added to the tension, and the one-minute silence to mark Winston Churchill's funeral that day was partly spoiled by the fans.

The match, played on a muddy quagmire of a pitch, was tough and uncompromising. Referee Howley was much too lenient and allowed dangerous play without taking action. As for the football; the defences were superb. The best chance in the first half fell to Everton's Pickering, after a ricochet off the referee, luckily for Leeds he shot wide with Sprake helpless.

Leeds began the second half brightly and were unlucky not to score when Charlton's header was cleared off the goal-line by Stevens. Leeds proceeded to launch attack after attack with the forwards cleverly switching positions. The pressure had to tell, and did on fifty-eight minutes when Storrie gleefully slammed a simple chance home after Johanesson's initial effort had struck a post.

Everton were in no mood to surrender and hit back immediately. Wright took a free kick; Sprake misjudged the flight off the cross and was beaten in the air by Gabriel who headed the ball towards goal. Whether the ball would have gone in is debatable, but Charlton took no chances and punched the ball away from under the bar. Pickering struck home the penalty.

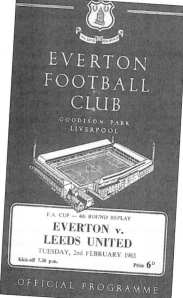

In the final quarter there was only one clear-cut chance. Fortunately for Leeds, Sprake atoned for his earlier error with a fine save from Wright. At the final whistle Everton were clearly the happier; Leeds knew they would face a formidable task in the replay.

Fourth Round Replay 2 February 1965

Everton	1 (0)	Pickering (82)
Leeds United	2 (0)	Charlton (73), Weston (80)

Attendance:	65,940
Receipts:	£14,834
Referee:	Mr K Howley (Billingham-on-Tees)

Everton: West, Wright, Wilson, Gabriel, Labone, Stevens, Scott, Harvey, Pickering, Temple, Morrissey
Leeds United: Sprake, Reaney, Bell, Bremner, Charlton, Hunter, Giles, Weston, Storrie, Collins, Cooper

Murky weather greeted the replay. Leeds made one change, Cooper for the unfit Johanesson. Despite the gothic atmosphere the game was faster, cleaner, and more open than the first. Both defences stood up well to intelligent play and during the early exchanges Everton held the upper hand with Scott, the playmaker, controlling the game. The best chances in this spell fell to Temple and Pickering, but both times Sprake saved magnificently. Leeds then began to feel their way into the game, and were unlucky not to score before the interval when both Cooper and Storrie had efforts well saved. The goalless first half had been exciting with neither side really deserving to be ahead.

In this topsy-turvy encounter Everton started the second period better. Harvey forced Sprake into a smart save with a fine header, then Scott drove the ball just wide of the far post. Pickering and Temple strove to break the deadlock, but Sprake was inspired and continually came to Leeds rescue. Having weathered this storm Leeds came back strongly, and slightly against the run of play took the lead in the seventy-third minute when Charlton leapt high above a crowd of players to power home a Giles centre. Leeds knew they had the edge and it was no surprise when seven minutes later they scored again. Bremner pushed the ball through to Weston, who turned Wright before driving the ball low past a despairing West.

Though Leeds were two goals ahead they were not allowed to relax. Within two minutes of the restart Pickering gave his side a lifeline converting Morrisey's delightful cross. The crowd was now in a frenzy. The goal not only galvanised Everton but also stirred Leeds, who just held on to their slender lead with grit, determination, and at times the run of the ball. At the final whistle no neutral could deny Leeds had deserved their victory. Sprake especially deserved praise, he had responded magnificently to pre-match criticism with four world class saves. For United to go to Goodison Park and come away with a victory in front of over 60,000 passionate fans was a tremendous achievement.

Fifth Round   20 February 1965

Leeds United	2(1) Giles (pen 29), Johanesson (80)
Shrewsbury	0(0)
Attendance:	47,740

Receipts: £13,250
Referee: Mr G Grundy (Grimsby)

Leeds United: Sprake, Reaney, Bell, Bremner, Charlton, Hunter, Giles, Weston, Storrie, Collins, Johanesson
Shrewsbury: Boswell, Wright, Wall, Hemsley, Dolby, Brodie, Meredith, Ross, Broadbent, Broadman, Taylor

After their magnificent display at Goodison it was a little surprising that for long periods Leeds struggled to break down a brave but average defence. In the end Bobby Collins made the difference; he was magnificent. The opening goal in this scrappy encounter came from a mix-up in Shrewsbury's defence when Storrie won possession. His initial shot was blocked by Boswell (Shrewsbury's goalkeeper), but the rebound fell kindly to Johanesson who would have opened the scoring but for Dolby handling the ball on the line. Giles sent Boswell the wrong way from the resultant spot kick.

Leeds may have been ahead but seemed lethargic and allowed the underdogs a greater share of possession. Indeed the visitors carved out a great chance, but Broadbent's good work came to nothing when none of his colleagues could finish off his efforts. Leeds went into the interval one goal to the good.

The second half was more one sided with the home side firmly in control. Eventually a second goal came with Collins inevitably the architect. After winning possession he struck a wonderful drive against the post, the ball rebounded straight to Johanesson who tucked the chance away to double the lead. Shrewsbury matched Leeds' bravery, work rate and heart, but had no cutting edge. Leeds were in the sixth round for only the second time in their short history. The city was beginning to buzz; Wembley was now only two wins away.

Sixth Round   10 March 1965

Crystal Palace   0(0)
Leeds United   3(0)   Peacock (58,68) Storrie (73)

Attendance: 45,384
Receipts: £14,639
Referee: Mr J Finney (Hereford)

Crystal Palace: Millington, Howe, Whitehouse, Petchey, Stephenson, Holsgrove, Horobin, Burnside, Holton, Smith, Kellard
Leeds United: Sprake, Reaney, Bell, Bremner, Charlton, Hunter, Giles, Storrie, Peacock, Collins, Cooper

Without having played at their best Leeds found themselves clear favourites to reach the semi-finals for the first time in the club's history. The draw took them to Selhurst Park for a tough looking tie against Crystal Palace. Due to adverse weather the scheduled game was postponed, but the home side were not complaining because the delay enabled Petchey and Burnside to return. Leeds made one change, Cooper again deputising for the injured Johanesson.

The packed crowd was to witness a bruising encounter. Palace, clearly fired up for the occasion by their manager, conceded twenty-nine fouls in all. They appeared desperate to upset the rhythm of the blue-shirted Leeds side. United were not intimidated and gave as good as they got, meeting every tackle with an even tougher one. If Palace wanted a battle so be it. The opening was all hustle and bustle, with few chances. Leeds worried the Palace keeper with long high lobs, but in turn looked shaky in the face of neat approach work from Holsgrove, Smith and Kellard. United had the best opportunity on forty minutes when Peacock's cross-shot just evaded Storrie. In truth it was a disappointing opening period.

The second half began with commitment again outshining skill. Then Leeds stepped up a gear and put the game beyond Palace with three goals in fifteen minutes. The first on fifty-eight minutes came from deep. Reaney, boxed in near his corner flag, cleverly worked his way forward, ably assisted by Giles. His final cross was perfect for Peacock to blast home. The crucial second arrived on sixty-eight minutes. Cooper intercepted a bad pass from Palace's defence; his quick ball was picked up by Peacock who again finished clinically. The game was all but over and five minutes later Leeds made sure with a third, this time Storrie converting Cooper's cross. Leeds iron, self-discipline had been crucial against a hard and cynical side. They were now in new territory; the last four of the FA Cup.

Semi Final 27 March 1965 at Hillsborough

Leeds United   0(0)
Manchester U.   0(0)

Attendance: 65,000

Receipts: £32,413
Referee: Mr R Windle (Chesterfield)

Leeds United: Sprake, Reaney, Bell, Bremner, Charlton J, Hunter, Giles, Storrie, Peacock, Collins, Johanesson
Manchester Utd: Dunne P, Brennan, Dunne A, Crerand, Foulkes, Stiles, Connelly, Charlton B, Herd, Law, Best

The semi final draw paired together the two teams vying for the league title; it was a match everybody wanted to see. Not surprisingly all 65,000 tickets were immediately snapped up. The match was bitterly contested; more remembered for its confrontations than open play. It was an ill-tempered maul on a sticky pitch that sapped stamina, and at times appeared to be played in slow motion. This was not a match for the faint hearted; it was raw blood and guts and the fans loved it.

Referee Windle's leniency was undoubtedly the major reason for this bad-tempered spectacle. How Law, Stiles and Bremner were the only players booked was incredible. The worst incident saw the referee lose total control after Law had chopped down Jack Charlton. There were angry exchanges, swinging fists and thrusting heads as both sides joined in a free-for-all. To cap it all when Bremner and Crerand tried to restore order they were the only ones lectured by Windle; Law getting away scot-free. Whilst Leeds were no angels there could be no doubt who the aggressors were.

What little football was played centred on Collins. His prompting allowed Peacock to go close with a header and an overhead kick, and Jack Charlton to force a desperate save from Crerand on the line. When the mood took them Manchester played some neat football and had the best chances throughout. However, Law and Bobby Charlton were well marshalled by Bremner and Hunter, and their flying wingers, Connelly and Best, were well shackled by Bell and Reaney. Sprake was effective when called on, and one save from Bobby Charlton was particularly memorable. In many ways the final whistle was a relief for all. The match may have ended goalless but the unsavoury incidents dominated the back pages ensuring even greater interest in the replay.

Semi Final Replay 31 March 1965 at The City Ground

Manchester U. 0(0)
Leeds United   1(0)   Bremner (88)

Attendance: 46,300
Receipts: £19,550
Referee: Mr R Windle (Chesterfield)

Manchester Utd: Dunne P, Brennan, Dunne A, Crerand, Foulkes, Stiles, Connelly, Charlton B, Herd, Law, Best
Leeds United: Sprake, Reaney, Bell, Bremner, Charlton J, Hunter, Giles, Storrie, Peacock, Collins, Cooper

Four days after 'The battle of Hillsborough' the only player unable to make the replay was Johanesson; Cooper again deputising. The change allowed Leeds more defensive cover in midfield where Crerand had been Manchester's most influential player in the first game. 46,000 fans packed the stadium hoping for a more open contest; they weren't to be disappointed. Even referee Windle took credit, taking a firm line from the start most fouls were technical not cynical. The tie was also helped with a change in playing conditions, a fast dry surface replacing thick sticky mud. Quality players were able to perform, and did.

Manchester began the game as if Leeds were in for a hiding. Early on Leeds were indebted to Sprake who made fine saves from Hird and Bobby Charlton. Leeds held firm and on sixteen minutes were a shade unlucky not to take the lead when Jack Charlton saw an effort strike the underside of the bar before being cleared to safety. Shortly after Bremner and Storrie's clever interchange nearly set up Peacock, but Brennan intercepted. Manchesters' best chance of the half fell to Bobby Charlton, who after side-stepping Bremner unleashed a thunderous shot that Sprake did well to save. Neither side was able to find a clear opening in the remaining minutes of the half, and though Manchester had shaded possession there were still no goals.

It is difficult to remember a more one-sided second period, Manchester were so on top during the first thirty minutes that Leeds at times looked desperate. Sprake thwarted Law and Best; Hird drove into the side netting, and then with a clear sight of goal unbelievably missed from ten yards out. It seemed inevitable that Manchester would score but Leeds dug deep and held on. The entire defence stood firm, repelling any danger to their goal, and behind them Sprake was inspired, dominating his area.

Any normal side would have been battered into submission, but not Leeds. Astonishingly as the game entered the final minutes Leeds started to fight back. Three times Dunne was forced to turn the ball over his bar, the last from a stunning Cooper volley. Next Leeds peppered the six-yard box with five successive corners but could not force the ball home. Then with barely two minutes remaining Stiles obstructed Giles, giving away a free kick. Giles settled himself before sending a deep cross from forty yards out into the heart of Manchester's goalmouth. The first to react was one of the smallest players on the field, Billy Bremner, who with his back to goal twisted and sent a backward header flashing into the top corner of the goal. Immediately a joyous procession raced after the ecstatic goal scorer to celebrate by the corner flag (Figure 3).

Moments later the final whistle signalled unbridled joy for the white rose team, and despair for their brave opponents. After forty-five years in the football wilderness Leeds United had finally arrived. It was a historic moment for the club reaching Wembley and the entire squad and backroom staff were determined to savour the moment.

Shortly after the triumph Revie said:

> *It was the proudest moment in all my career when the whistle went last night and Leeds United were in the Cup Final. My deepest thanks to the team for a magnificent display of football and courage - and to every player on our staff, for they all helped to remake the club.* [5]

Goal hero Bremner added:

> *I cannot remember a lot about the goal. I just darted in, seeing a little opening, and headed the ball through the only gap I could see. But immediately I saw it in the net I think I went delirious.*

Figure 3. Storrie lifts Bremner high in the air after scoring the goal that took Leeds to their first FA Cup Final. *Photograph used courtesy of Yorkshire Evening Post Newspapers*

Certainly my eyes were full of tears of joy.[6]

Chairman Harry Reynolds said:

'I was delighted to receive the congratulations of Manchester United's directors and of Mr Matt Busby, their famous manager, who I may say hoped that we would win the Cup.[7]

Bobby Collins recalled the two games:

The first game was a bit naughty, but that was caused by them they started things. The replay was really something. The goal I remember because I was going to take the free kick near the end but Johnny insisted on taking it, and Billy headed it in a for the winning goal. After the game the atmosphere in the dressing room was absolutely wonderful. We knew we were going to Wembley to play in the Cup Final, the first time the club had achieved it, it was brilliant. We stayed at Grantham that night and I had to carry my room mate to bed! It was a terrific night. Everyone connected with the club, players and supporters, were just so happy.[8]

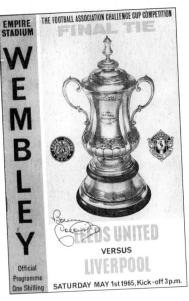

FINAL 1 May 1965 at Wembley Stadium

| Leeds United | 1(0) | Bremner (101) |
| Liverpool 2(0) | | Hunt (93), St John (111) |

Attendance:	100,000
Receipts:	£89,103
Referee:	Mr W Clements
	(West Bromwich)

Leeds United: Sprake, Reaney, Bell, Bremner, Charlton, Hunter, Giles, Storrie, Peacock, Collins, Johanesson

Liverpool: Lawrence, Lawler, Byrne, Strong, Yeats, Stevenson, Callaghan, Hunt, St John, Smith, Thompson

Shortly before 3.00pm on a wet and miserable May day, Don Revie and Bill Shankly led their teams out at Wembley before 100,000 noisy spectators. For Leeds United it was a hugely proud moment, their first FA Cup Final. The skippers, Bobby Collins and Ron Yates, introduced their colleagues to the

Duke of Edinburgh before getting down to the main event (Figure 4).

In an uneventful first half defences were on top with each side keeping eight men behind the ball at all times; it was ultra defensive. The best chance in the opening period fell to Hunt who had a blistering shot turned over the bar by Sprake. Leeds were clearly below par, prone to sub-standard passing and showed little inspiration. The action was not living up to the pre-match hype.

In the second half again defences dominated and persistent rain continued to make ball control difficult. As the game progressed Liverpool began to dictate; Thompson shot wide, Callaghan drove into the side netting and St John headed over when well placed. Liverpool were having their best spell and Leeds were indebted to Sprake who kept them in the game with wonderful saves from Thompson and St John. Leeds hardly had a worthy shot to mention and were doing all the chasing. To make matters worse Storrie was

Figure 4. Bobby Collins (right) and Ron Yeats shake hands before the Cup Final at Wembley. *Photograph used courtesy of Yorkshire Evening Post Newspapers*

hobbling badly, clearly a passenger. As full time approached Sprake once again came to Leeds rescue with two more saves, this time from Thompson and Smith. It seemed that only Liverpool could win, but even they could not manage it in the ninety minutes so the match went to extra time for the first time since 1947.

Finally the incessant rain took its toll and as tiredness affected the players, goals arrived in an action packed extra time period. After only three minutes the deadlock was broken; not surprisingly Liverpool took the lead when Roger Hunt converted Byrne's cross. With their confidence high Liverpool scented victory, and Byrne and St John brought more excellent saves from Sprake. Leeds looked finished but somehow forced their weary legs into attack, and eight minutes after conceding a goal equalised. Peacock initially found Hunter in midfield, Charlton headed on his cross to Bremner twelve yards out, the little Scot then instinctively let fly with a wonderful volley that scorched into the net (Figure 5).

Unfortunately for Leeds followers the equaliser galvanised Liverpool, constant possession finally told nine minutes from time when St John reacted first to Callaghan's cross to head the winning goal. There was no way back for Leeds now, indeed Liverpool nearly increased their lead through Thompson and Smith. At the end there could be no denying Liverpool deserved their victory. After the game Revie shook the hands of every player, he knew his side had been well beaten but was still proud.

So it was not to be, Leeds United ultimately failed in their two-pronged assault on English football's two major domestic competitions. Although the season ended in failure, more importantly thousands of Leeds supporters knew their team had finally risen above the mediocrity of the past and a solid foundation was now in place for the glory that would become known as the 'Revie years' (Figure 6).

The final word must go to the captain himself, Bobby Collins

(Figure 7), who recalled his own personal memories of that season's campaign:

> *Before the 1964/65 season people were talking about Leeds United going down, not staying up. At the start teams underestimated us, but we were in really good shape and if we went a goal up it was very rare we lost.*
>
> *Two league games in particular stand out. In both the referee took us off the pitch, but for different reasons. Against Everton at Goodison Sandy Brown punched Johnny Giles in the first minute and got sent off. We scored the only goal in the first half...I took a free kick and flipped one in... 'boomph' Willie Bell scored with a header. The tackles were flying in and a section of the crowd threw their cushions on the field. That was one of the most ferocious games I ever played in. Later that season we played Manchester United at Old Trafford. The fog came down and was getting worse when Jim Finney [the referee], took us off. Fortunately the mist cleared enough for us to finish the game. I scored the only goal; some people probably didn't see it. It was a great result.*

Figure 5. Bremner equalises for Leeds with a stunning volley, unfortunately it wasn't enough. *Photograph used courtesy of Yorkshire Evening Post Newspapers*

By then we were vying for the title with United and it stayed that way till the end of the season. Losing on goal average was hard to take; maybe it would have been better if there had been a play-off, but nevertheless we'd done really well.

It was a heavy week before the final at Wembley, we played

Figure 6. The Leeds United side that played in the Cup Final. *Back Row* (L-R): Hunter, Charlton, Sprake, Reaney, Bell. *Front Row* (L-R): Giles, Storrie, Peacock, Revie (Manager), Collins (Captain), Johanesson, Bremner.
Photograph used courtesy of Yorkshire Evening Post Newspapers

Sheffield on the Saturday and Birmingham on the Monday, then went straight to London to prepare. As for the match itself...well to be fair, I was Player of the Year that season...but I wouldn't have won the award if I'd played like I did at Wembley. I never seemed to get in the game at all. Unfortunately we had one guy who froze, one injured, and that made it hard work for the nine left. Having said that, Billy scored a fantastic goal. I wish we'd have survived extra time because I think we'd have had it over them in the replay.

When you get beat in a final it's very hard to come up with words that will soothe anybody. Yes we had a wonderful time at the hotel afterwards, with a nice banquet, but it would have been much better if we had won. The bus ride through the city was great; thousands of fans turned out (Figure 8).

Figure 7. Bobby Collins was arguably the most important signing that Don Revie ever made. His influence and experience was crucial as the club embarked on the greatest period in their history. *Photograph used courtesy of Yorkshire Evening Post Newspapers*

Figure 8. Though Leeds lost the Final, their supporters were proud of the club's achievements that season, and thousands welcomed them home.
Photograph used courtesy of Yorkshire Evening Post Newspapers

To lose the League on goal difference and the Cup in extra time was a fantastic achievement; Leeds had never achieved anything like that before. The highlight of the season for me was when Billy scored the winning goal against Manchester United in the semi final. You can never change a first and that goal meant Leeds were in an FA Cup final for the first time in their history. It was the most fantastic season, one of the greatest of my career.[9]

Notes and References

1 Jason Thomas, *The Leeds United Story*, Arthur Barker Limited, 1971, p13.
2 Eric Thornton, *Leeds United & Don Revie*, Robert Hale & Company, 1970, pp 65-7.
3 Jason Thomas, *The Leeds United Story*, Arthur Barker Limited, 1971, p16.
4 David Saffer and Howard Dapin, *Leeds United Cup Kings 1972*, Bluecoat Press, 1998, p7.
5 *Yorkshire Evening Post -Cup Final Souvenir - Wembley at last!*, 26.4.65,p11.
6 *ibid*
7 *ibid*
8 Interview with Bobby Collins, April 1998
9 Interview with Bobby Collins, April 1998

Further Reading

For Leeds and England - Jackie Charlton, Stanley Paul, 1967.
Forward With Leeds - Johnny Giles, Stanley Paul, 1970.
You Get Nowt For Being Second - Billy Bremner, Souvenir Press, 1970.
Don Warters, *Leeds United - The Official History of the Club*, Wensum Books (Norwich) Ltd, 1979.
Andrew Mourant, *Don Revie - Portrait of a Footballing Enigma*, Mainstream Publishing, 1990.
Martin Jarred and Malcolm Macdonald, *The Leeds United Cup Book*, Breedon Books Sport, 1991.
Andrew Mourant, *Leeds United - The Glory Years,* The Bluecoat Press.
Martin Jarred and Malcolm Macdonald, *The Leeds United Story*, Breedon Books Sport, 1992.
Martin Jarred and Malcolm Macdonald, *Leeds United- A Complete Record*, Breedon Books Sport, 1996.

Acknowledgements

Our sincere thanks to Bobby Collins for recalling his memories of this period. We would also like to thank Leeds United FC, Everton FC, Crystal Palace FC, Sheffield Wednesday FC, Nottingham Forest FC and Wembley Plc for allowing us access to their match programmes.

Finally, we are indebted to the *Yorkshire Evening Post* for supplying all the photographs.

2. Variety Spells Entertainment: The Cinema Life of Claude H Whincup

by Robert E Preedy

Figure 1: Claude H Whincup...from Silents to Cinemascope.
Courtesy of R C Whincup

CLAUDE H WHINCUP HAD A LIFE SPANNING all the significant developments in the cinematographic trade. He worked through the 'silent' age and took his cinema chain into the 1930s 'sound' era. He kept the projectors running through the dark days of the war, and later in life battled against the unstoppable audience decline of the post war years. From the early forties he was also a leading light in the Exhibition Trade Association and achieved the accolade of National President in 1954. During his time in office he was always described by contemporaries as a statesman and gentleman (Figure 1).

Claude H Whincup was born into the cinema trade. His father ran a cinema in Lancashire from 1908, quickly establishing a film distribution company, Feature Films Ltd, based in Blackburn. A Yorkshire office opened in Leeds after the war and it was from here that Claude began working with his father. To increase his experience, he took a job as assistant to the Circuit Manager with Provincial Cinematograph Theatres in 1922. His base was the *Picture House* in Briggate (later known as the *Rialto*, now the site of Marks and Spencers). A year later Claude rejoined his father, becoming film booker for their newly acquired cinema, the *Grand Picture House* in York. By 1928, Claude was manager of the *Tower* and *Carlton* cinemas, Leeds forming part of the expanding Associated Tower Cinemas group, a company incorporated in 1920 by Walter Ellis and G W Watson to bring together cinema interests in Hull and Goole with their newly opened *Tower* cinema in Briggate.

By the late twenties, experiments with sound pictures began exciting the audience but the *Tower* held the claim of being the last Leeds city centre stronghold of silent films (Figure 2). 'Talkies are not screened here, only the best silent pictures accompanied by a human symphony orchestra under the direction of Bensley Ghent', stated Claude in 1929. However , within a few months the supply of silent films dried up and by March 1930 the *Tower* was re-equipped and screened its first talkie, a Mickey Mouse cartoon. The *Carlton* was also updated for sound in June 1930.

During this summer of 1930, Claude set sail on a fact-finding mission to North America. Here he was hugely impressed by the enterprise of American and Canadian cinemas. Many had late night film shows, an attractive pricing policy and a warm welcome for patrons. Equally he was saddened by some slack business caused in equal parts by the financial crash, poor films and very hot weather. On Claude's return to the UK, he quickly added another screen to the Associated Tower group, the *Stanningley Pavilion* which was rapidly equipped for sound from December 1930.[1]

Figure 2: An early 1920's scene outside the Tower Cinema, Briggate featuring an intriguing appearance by Leeds girl Stella Muir.
Courtesy of R C Whincup

In August 1932 Claude was married to Janet Whitley Gill of Summerbridge, Harrogate. Also in the early thirties Claude was promoted to Secretary and General Manager of Associated Tower Cinemas. The company's next take-over was of the Capitol Cinema in Meanwood in May 1934.

The latter half of the decade saw rapid changes in the exhibition trade. The future effect of television was a talking point as early as 1935. Technicolor was used from April 1936, the same year that some suburban Halls began using gifts and competitions to induce patronage. Different programming formats were tested as competition increased. The *Tower* cinema held a repertory week showing a different older film every day. Although the artistic experience was outstanding, the box office success proved less so. Within the trade it became apparent that by 1937 there were too many cinemas in Leeds. Each new supercinema consigned an older suburban Hall to a lingering death. One owner even proposed erecting a new Hall within a short distance of his existing cinema. Frank Thompson, the owner of the Golden Acre Amusement Park, wished to build a more modern cinema at the corner of St Anne's Road and Otley Road, Headingley. His *Cottage Road Picture House* would then be closed. Luckily the council opposed the idea and the 1912 *Headingley Picture House*, Cottage Road, continues to prosper as an Associated *Tower* cinema.[2]

During 1936 Claude extended his empire by taking the post of Director of British Cinematograph Theatres Ltd, with Halls in the South of England at Felixstowe and Caterham. This group grew under Claude's control and by the late fifties included screens in Golders Green, Enfield and Tottenham. Another enterprise from 1938 saw Claude Whincup in charge of a small chain being built in Pocklington, Driffield and Pickering.[3]

Wartime added extra worries to the operation of cinemas, and in 1941 Claude was elected Chairman of the Leeds Branch of the Cinema Exhibitors Association. Within a year of this appointment a film product shortage allowed distributors to increase their rental on top pictures to an unprecedented 50 per cent of box office; a figure possibly acceptable on first run, but months later on third run was uneconomic for smaller suburban Halls.

Another issue was the Sunday opening of cinemas which was talked about in Leeds from 1943. Many cinemas were against it because of labour shortages, plus the imposition of a financial clause forcing owners to donate some of the evening's takings to charity. Other towns such as Harrogate, Wakefield, Ripon, Sheffield, York

Figure 3: An amazing queue around the picture house and down through the Grand Arcade (still owned by Associated Tower group).

Courtesy of R C Whincup

and Scarborough sanctioned Sunday opening much earlier than Leeds. Eventually a public referendum in March 1946, confirmed seven day opening in Leeds cinemas.[4]

One of the most compelling arguments in favour, was that it gave young people a place to frequent on Sunday, a traditionally quiet trading day. Christmas Day opening had been normal in Leeds since 1926, but was abandoned in 1946, a combination of trade union resistance and an admission that the day was never that good for business.

Some years earlier, in 1943, the CEA was asked whether cinemas should open on Armistice Night. The authorities were keen to relieve congestion on the streets but cinemas worried about exuberant patrons damaging seats.

During the war, cinema admissions increased to unprecedented levels. By 1944 (the year AT took over the *Crescent*, Dewsbury Road), these amounted to 30 million a week (Figure 3). With a keen eye on tax revenue, the government increased the Entertainment Tax at the same time as boosting the British Film Quota.

The Entertainment Tax had been introduced in 1917 as a temporary measure 'to be abolished after the war' yet by 1938 the tax was draining cinemas of £5.6 million or 16 percent of turnover. Within nine years the tax had been increased by 700 percent to extract an incredible £41 million (33 per cent of box office takings). This tax burden combined with the increase in film rentals meant that although income was at an all time high, many cinemas

Figure 4. The Headingley Picture House, Number 3 Cottage Road, pictured in 1949. On screen this week the film 'Bitter Rice' an Italian social drama about the exploitation of rice-field workers in the Po Valley. Coming shortly is the Ivor Novello operetta set in the Austrian Alps *The Dancing Years*. *Author's collection*

were operating on very thin margins. The battle had begun between the high street giants and the vulnerable independents.

The threat of television started to grow in the late forties. American cinemas had been decimated since the first stateside television transmissions in 1947. Over six thousand screens closed within three years. Here in the UK the BBC offered to publicise cinemas by screening a weekly half hour trailers programme broadcast from a northern cinema.

Behind the scenes cinemas were reeling from the cost of showing pictures of the Royal Wedding in December 1947. From a normal charge of £5 per week, the Regal wedding cost cinemas a staggering £60.

In the same month, the big circuits were given an exclusive six week run on all new films. The independents faced the prospects of screening 'played out' pictures.

Also in 1947 an even bigger threat was unveiled. As a possible solution to the balance of payments crisis, J Arthur Rank was approached by the government to increase his studio output. To give these British pictures a chance to compete with stateside releases, the British Film Quota was increased to 45 per cent. Consequently virtually all of Rank's output had to be booked and a new monopoly emerged due to Rank's control of the *Odeon* and *Gaumont* circuits. To add to the restrictions, Rank proposed charging a 50 per cent film rental. The American producers reacted angrily to the Quota and demanded screen exclusivity; their pictures were not to be used as support 'B' films.

Yet more misery was awaiting the cinemas when the Eady Plan became law in 1950. This was a tax on the seat price and was designed to be used to support British film production. Claude Whincup and the CEA faced an impossible battle when all these factors conspired to spell the end of the cinema era. Twenty years of these millstones and the start of television in 1949 in London (from October 1951 in the north) meant the sad end for hundreds of small neighbourhood Halls. By 1953 Claude was elected Vice President of the CEA and the following year he became the President, but the battles hardly became easier.

To offer the public a novel experience, new widescreen pictures began to appear in the early fifties. The first *The Robe*, from the giant Fox Film Company, required a massive new screen and a three speaker stereo sound system, a massive investment for a small cinema. But within fifteen months, nearly a thousand cinemas were re-equipped. Claude Whincup sounded a note of caution, and was proved correct. These improvements produced little extra box-office

Figures 5 and 6: The traditional interior of the Cottage Road cinema prior to modernisation in 1972. The picture house, originally owned by Owen Brooks and George Reginald Smith, opened on Monday 29th July 1912 with continuous film performances from 6 to 10 pm. Admission then was 6d or one shilling for a reserved seat. The cinema was taken over by the Associated Tower group in 1938. The original seating of 590 has been reduced over the years to the present number 468. *Author's collection*

revenue (Figure 5 and 6).

A few years later some renters started to sell their films to television, doing the industry a 'dis-service' in Claude's words. Another attack was proposed for exhibitors, some renters threatened to demand details of ancillary sales, in order to assess an exhibitor's financial position.

The mid-fifties continued to bring gloom to the local cinemas. Between 1954 and 1959 attendances halved. Fewer American films entered the country because of the Quota system and during this squeeze film renters introduced a new method of payment; 'break figures' (a certain percentage up to an agreed figure, then a higher percentage after that). Today this system seems fair, but to cinemas facing bankruptcy in the fifties it was viewed as another way of extracting extra revenue from the box office.

As President of the CEA for the year 1954-1955, Claude witnessed the total transformation of the industry. Small cinemas closed in their hundreds, while the chains increased their grip on trade by exploiting their first run monopoly, effectively keeping top films away from the vulnerable independents. The cinema business was always built on the drum roll of publicity, but in the fifties all patrons heard about, was decline.

In 1957 the Associated Tower group diversified away from cinemas with the purchase of the *Astoria Ballroom* in Roundhay Road.

During his period of office, Claude was regarded as a true diplomat, avoiding as best he could, direct confrontation with the film renters. It was reported that he 'stood his ground with tenacity in a chaotic period for cinemas.'

Claude H Whincup died aged fifty-eight in November 1962 after a long illness. His forty year career in the business encompassed the golden years of the cinema industry.

Notes and References

1. The Headingley *Lounge* Cinema opened in 1916 and was not owned by Associated Tower until 1970.
2. The Headingley *Cottage Road* Picture House is one of only a handful of cinemas across the country still operating from this period.
3. The 386 seater *Castle* Cinema, Pickering was operated by the author for eight years from 1984.
4. The vote was 62, 962 for and 25,138 against on a 25 per cent turnout.

Acknowledgements

The author acknowledges the invaluable help with this article from Claude H Whincup's son, Richard.

3. THOSE JAW BONES

by William H Banks

ACCORDING TO ONE REPORT, the bones became a landmark in 1835 when they were donated by a mine owning family named Fenton who had used them as gate posts at their Woodhouse Lane mansion. John Batty, in the History of Rothwell when describing the Bridle Stile or Park House Road from York to Manchester writes:

> *To proceed to Leeds: Instead of going down by the Green Engine take the road down to the Jaw Bones round the corner and down Bell Hill Lane, then merely a somewhat narrow lane down to Thwaite Gate.*

> *...They are really the Jaw Bones of a Whale, brought it is said from America by one of the Fentons and placed over the gateway of the Fentons House. They were fastened together with a beam at the top - the bolt holes can be seen yet. They were removed in Mr Harrison's time and placed as ordinary gate posts in their present position at the corner opposite the Guide Posts. Plainly they are getting less, the ends inserted in the ground decaying so that in a few years they will disappear all together.* [1]

Some further explanation is clearly needed. The Bridle Path referred to crossed the road known as Wood Lane and continued down what became known as Low Shops Lane at the top of which was a Pumping Engine named Green Engine. At that time the road down Bell Hill was little more than a narrow dirt track and the first set of Jaw Bones were placed on the road near to the Wood Lane junction.

The sinking and opening of Beeston Pit at the top of Bell Hill had some bearing on the siting of the bones in 1870, but the major road alteration of widening and strengthening came about in 1903. The erection of the tram sheds and the laying of tram tracks brought about the removal and a further re-siting of the bones over the Wood Lane footpath, complete with a gas lamp on top (Figure 1).

The first tram down Thwaite Gate was on the 3 August 1904 and a passenger service began on Monday 15 August 1904. Rothwell tramway began running passenger on 2 December 1904.

The bones were however suffering from decay, and were replaced with other bones through the action of Mr James Hargreaves, a member of the Rothwell Urban District Council for many years, and

Figure 1. Jaw Bones, Rothwell Haigh in the early nineteenth century. *Author's collection*

who was its Chairman three times from 1891-1893, 1897-1898 and 1903-1904. Mr Hargreaves was also prominent in the management of J & J Charlesworth Coal Mines.

The bones suffered serious damage when they were hit by a motor vehicle which bandits were using to try and escape from the police in 1932. For a short while Rothwell was without its famous landmark, but in January 1935, following an article in the *Evening Post*, developments took place.

Here is the article and appeal:

ROTHWELL PREPARED TO PAY £5 FOR A GOOD PAIR OF BONES.

WANTED A PAIR OF WHALE JAW BONES - GOOD CONDITION

I make this announcement on behalf of a responsible body, in fact a Local Government Body, Rothwell Urban District Council. Rothwell is crying 'alas and alack'. The famous whale jaw bones which stood near the tram sheds at Wood Lane, are no more. They were one of Rothwell's claims to fame, yet they have had to go, what was left of them. For a number of years prior to their demise, they supported a gas lamp over the pavement. Rothwell has had its whale jaw bones for well nigh 100 years. The tale which has such a sad ending began early in last century when a local farmer received from Hull a bonny pair of whale bones. He used them as gate posts on the present site, and so built a Rothwell tradition, besides a canny pair of gate posts.[2]

As a result of the *Yorkshire Evening Post* article, Mr E F Moorhouse, the Clerk of the Council, reported that an offer by Joseph Barraclough of Bankfield Mills, Mirfield to supply a pair of jaw bones at a cost of £3 10s was to hand. They had been in use as gate posts at Mirfield for about thirty years, and were in good condition and, unless wilfully damaged should last another 100 years. The bones were purchased and put in place in 1935.

The tramway development included a sub-station with an engineer, and a large waiting room with ample seating and a large fireplace together with office accommodation. There was also a large tram shed housing trams in for repair and a bogey equipped for breakdown repairs. The waiting room was provided initially to accommodate passengers travelling from Wakefield to Rothwell and

Figure 2. Electric tram depot and tram ticket from the last day of service. *Author's collection*

LEEDS CITY TRANSPORT DEPARTMENT

CROSS GATES, HALTON & TEMPLE NEWSAM TRAM SERVICES

THIS TICKET WAS ISSUED ON THE LAST DAY OF OPERATION, SATURDAY NOVEMBER 7th 1959, TO MARK THE CLOSING DOWN OF THE TRAMWAY SYSTEM IN LEEDS.

Fare 6d.

Figure 3. Whale jaw bones and St Georges 1969 Clower Tower - formerly Workhouse 1903. *Author's collection*

Figure 4. Whale jaw bones, Wood Lane End 1969. *Author's collection*

back. In both cases a change of vehicle took place at the Jaw Bones (Figure 2).

In the 1920s the waiting room was closed for short periods because of vandalism and intrusion by vagrants for whom it was a convenient resting place before entering the nearby Workhouse (Figure 3). Other misuses took place as well as damage and the people for whom the facility was provided were loathe to enter when tramps were in occupation. The change over from tramcars to buses brought about the final and permanent closure of the waiting room.

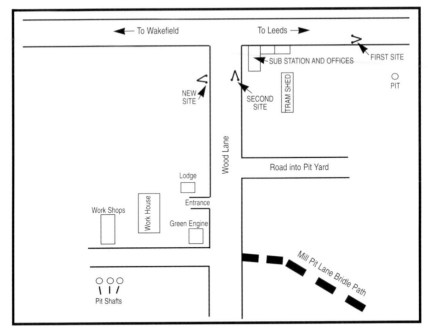

Figure 5. Map showing the various sites of the Whale Jaw Bones.
Author's collection

Alas and alack, the bones suffered damage in the mid 1960s and were eventually replaced in 1969, but re-sited on the opposite side of Wood Lane, and are still there (Figure 4 and 5).

Notes and References

1 Batty *History of Rothwell* facsimile reproduction of 1866 Almar Books Kirkstall Leeds p205-6
2 *Yorkshire Evening Post*, 8 January 1935

4. Growing Up in New Leeds

by Kathleen Gurney

CHAPELTOWN ROAD WAS CONSTRUCTED by John Metcalf, more commonly known as Blind Jack of Knaresborough, in 1750. About a hundred and thirty eight years later, both my parents were born and nurtured in the area alongside that road, which was situated between Potternewton and Sheepscar, and known as New Leeds. Here, extensive fields had once stretched, flanked by quarries and scrubland, as early maps show. Mention of New Leeds appears on the first edition of the one inch to one mile Ordnance Survey map of 1847-51, where Cowper Villa is marked on the top street of what was to become a grid of streets (Figure 1). Running down the right side is a wide road which developed into beautiful Spencer Place. Here, one or two houses and gardens are already set out. The lowest street on the grid would be Leopold Street, bordered on its left by Chapletown Road. A little way above the Sheepscar bar stood the Cavalry Barracks, built about 1820 at a cost of £28,000 and

Figure 1. Early Ordnance Survey map of 1847-51 showing proposed area of New Leeds. *Author's collection*

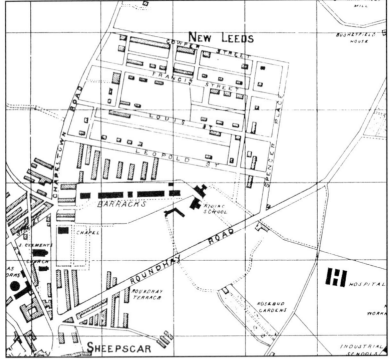

Figure 2. Ordnance Survey, 1866. *Author's collection*

Figure 3. St Clement's church, Chapeltown, reproduced from a programme October 1911.
Author's collection

positioned in what was then considered a healthy, country place, but they were later condemned by the Inspector General as 'the worst in all England'[1]

Although many more houses had been built by 1866, the Barracks remained much in evidence; their Riding School grounds extending beyond Roundhay Road and circled by a path leading to the Rosebud Gardens, which my maternal grandmother claimed to remember (Figure 2).

In 1866, the handsome church of St Clement's was built in Chapletown Road (Figure 3). Almost opposite, its Non-Conformist neighbour Roscoe Chapel, was said to be the first dissenting place of worship to be provided with a bell turret and bell (Figure 3).

The development of New Leeds and surrounding parts can be best seen on the six inch to one mile 1906 Ordnance Survey map of the area. The Godfrey reissue of this map is accompanied on the back by a history of the district and extracts from the Robinson's Street Directory of the time. My late father would have had pleasure in noting that 3 Leopold Street, his family home for many years, was occupied at this time by a Reverend W Shaw, who was curate-in-charge of St Luke's, North Street, a church erected originally for use by the soldiers of the Barracks.[2]

Chapeltown Road rose slightly uphill to the genteel streets of Potternewton, with its Reginalds and Sholebrokes, where at 63 Sholebroke Avenue lived the Reverend Arthur K Stowell, reminding one of Gordon Stowell's *Button Hill*, a novel set in those upper

Figure 4. Based on the Ordnance Survey of 1906, scale 1: 2500 (redrawn).

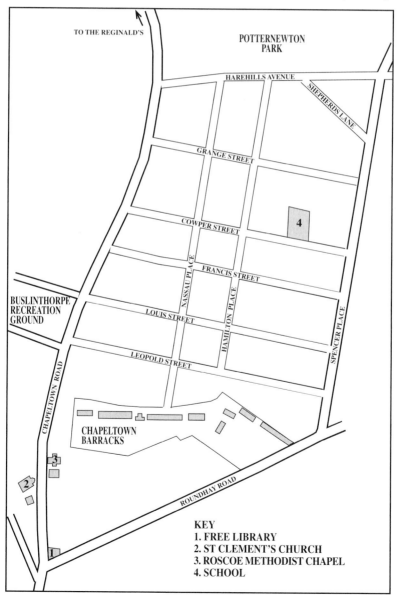

TO THE REGINALD'S

POTTERNEWTON PARK

HAREHILLS AVENUE

SHEPHERDS LANE

GRANGE STREET

COWPER STREET

4

FRANCIS STREET

NASSAU PLACE

BUSLINTHORPE RECREATION GROUND

LOUIS STREET

HAMILTON PLACE

SPENCER PLACE

LEOPOLD STREET

CHAPELTOWN ROAD

CHAPELTOWN BARRACKS

ROUNDHAY ROAD

KEY
1. FREE LIBRARY
2. ST CLEMENT'S CHURCH
3. ROSCOE METHODIST CHAPEL
4. SCHOOL

reaches, and very evocative of the time which my parents knew well.[3]

Although Stowell's streets remain, many parts of my family's location were demolished and replaced by modern buildings. Traffic streams down to the wide junction at Sheepscar, where in earlier days had stood a Police Station and Library. A busy new road system has now replaced the older layout. St Clement's was knocked down to make way for it, as were many little shops, one of which bore the enchanting name of Derewonko. Would it have been Mr Derewonko himself who could be seen through the upper window, busy with his pressing iron?

Families used to like living in close proximity to one another. My father's family lived at two addresses in Leopold Street, in Amberley Terrace, Nassau Place, Francis Street, Grange Avenue and later in Brandon Grove (Figure 4). Father's Father, Joseph Cooper, was organist and choirmaster at St Michael's, Buslingthorpe, and as a boy he attended St Michael's school. He wrote to his parents in 1872 ...

When I get old enough to work I hope to repay you in some degree for
Figure 5. Letter from Joseph Cooper to his parents dated 1872.
Authors collection

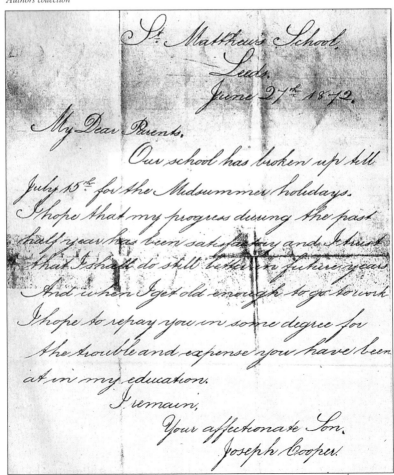

the trouble and expense you have been at in my education (Figure 5)[4.]

He was organist at Buslingthorpe for nine years until he died aged only thirty-six in 1896; a memorial window was erected for him in the church which now, alas, has been pulled down. His early death left a wife with six children on her hands, but her father and mother -in-law supported her financially, and took the eldest child to live with them in Amberley Terrace. This was Harry, later to become my father (Figure 6).

Mother's family, however, were not surrounded by relatives, for they were all left behind in Almondbury, near Huddersfield, when Joseph Dickinson obtained a post, also as organist and choirmaster, at Newton Park Union Congregationalist Church in Chapeltown. He brought his young wife and two children to Leeds in 1870, and held a post at the church for twenty-one years. He was also an able performer on both violin and piano, and took about twenty or thirty pupils for music lessons. In what little spare time he had, he managed to build in his attic a small pipe organ. In later years, two of his

Figure 6. Cooper family. (Date c. 1912) Standing, left to right, Harry Cooper, and Clifton. Seated, Fanny Louisa Cooper.

Figure 7. Dickinson Family. Date unknown. Standing, Joseph Clark Dickinson. 2nd row, left to right, John Arthur, George, Hannah with Alfred on lap, James William. 3rd row, Mary Eliza, Harry.

sons followed their father's career, William as organist at St Columba's Buslingthorpe (known as *Tin Heaven*), and Alfred at St Joseph's Primitive Methodist Church, where he earned a princely £10 a year, playing an organ which had amber keys in place of some black ones. This organ was, of course, hand pumped. Alfred told a story about the fellow who was blowing for the *Hallelujah Chorus*, and the wind gave out three bars from the mighty end. When rebuked for this neglect, he replied with spirit 'Ah've blown fo't Allelujah this last fifteen year, and Ah knaws 'ow many pumps to give it!'[5]

As the years passed, the Dickinson family grew from two children to seven (Figure 7). Mama was a very kindly woman who had instituted a custom for Sunday dinnertime. Maggie, their little maid of all work, would come into the dining room and say, 'Please, Missus, the little ragged boys are here', whereupon both the parents and all the children would remove onto two plates an untouched portion of their good roast meal; and Maggie would take this bounty to the two poor little boys, who ate it outside in a shed.

'They are God's children' declared Mama. Dada was rather Bohemian in his weekday dress of cloak and soft black hat, but he was by no means soft on discipline. An oft used expression was 'Do as your told, or you'll think an elephant has kicked you!' All save the two girls in the family were given 'good hidings' for any misdemeanour. John Arthur, the eldest, got a special whacking after

Figure 8. Family tree. *Author's collection*

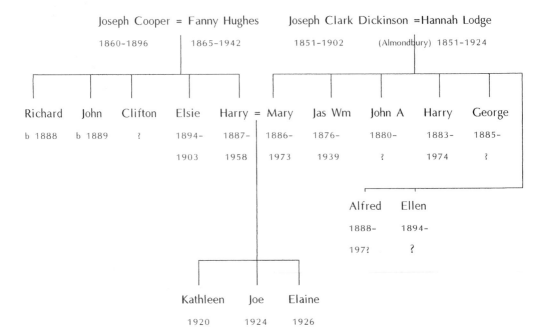

he had stood at the doorway of Roscoe Place Chapel, shouting that he would knock off the stone head of John Wesley, whose image, with other notables, adorned the chapel doorway. J A swung his walking stick at the head, but managed only to de-nose it; and so it remained until Roscoe was demolished in the days of modernisation.

Shortly after I was born in 1920, my parents and I were transferred to 3 Leopold Street, which accommodated not only Grannie and ourselves, but also two other sons: Dick and his wife, and wayward Clifton, who slept in the attic (Figure 8). Built some time after 1860, these houses were commodious and tall. At number 3, one walked up some broad stone steps to a heavy front door adorned with a great amber glass knob, nicely faceted, but not made of golden toffee, as I had once thought. A long, narrow garden contained a lawn and flower beds where Lily of the Valley and Solomon's Seal struggled under some small trees by the gate, which opened and shut with a rusty squeal. Beyond the front door was a hall floored with coloured tiles, and the stairs ascended straight up to a half landing with a tall window bordered with red and blue glass. The remaining stairs led to four or five bedrooms, a cold bathroom, and a wc with a blue-patterned bowl under its mahogany seat. A mysterious door opened onto the attic stairway. When very small, I used to be held up to look out of a small window up there.

'Can you see Sugarwell...and the Seven Sisters?' they used to say. I couldn't, and what they were telling me seemed strange and magical, and the Seven Sisters were not trees, as once they were, but faraway fairy brides. Solid blocks of houses hug the treeless hill today.

Downstairs, there were bay windows seeming miles high, screened by shutters, wooden Venetian blinds, lace drapery and thick wool curtains. Marble mantelpieces held glittering glass spikes, waxen flowers under domes, china dogs, little men with nodding heads, whilst in fireplace alcoves lurked ceramic handled bell pushes, not to be touched. From the back door a flight of stone steps went down to cold stone cellars, but the

Figure 9. Social programme showing a forthcoming attraction and an advertisement.
Author's collection

Figure 10. Camping, 1914. Harry Cooper is on the left.

kitchen along a flagged passage was warm and redolent of carbolic soap. In the yard outside, a circular metal plate hid a coal chute. High brick walls enclosed this yard, the walls of which were topped with vicious shards of broken glass: a deterrent then commonplace and acceptable.

Social activities were centred round church or chapel, where friendships and romance blossomed. I think my parents met at a church bazaar. Bazaars were run by ladies in their best hats, which were not removed indoors. There were concerts, talks, sewing circles, homely soirees (Figure 9). At home, there was above all, the great Christmas Family Gathering, when the man of the house 'carved', to the accompaniment of such admiring cries as 'Oh, Willie! What a beautiful bird!' (meaning the turkey over which his knife was poised), and tots of home made rhubarb wine fit to stun the company were raised in toasts.

Young men like my father engaged in such pursuits as billiards, bridge, tennis (after a good walk up to the Street Lane courts), football and cricket. Sporting heroes were collected in postcard form, together with pictures of popular actresses. Even now Miss Gabriel Ray still resides in our postcard box, along with some cricket men.

Mother's five brothers were made to do Sandow muscle building exercises every morning, swinging heavy iron dumb-bells. Long rambles were taken, as my father's 1906 diary tells, 'Took young Clifton for a walk to Adel and the Seven Arches'.[6] He also mentions cycling to Bridlington and back. Camping in a field on Street Lane was also enjoyed, or endured, frying bacon outside the tent in the morning air (Figure 10).

As a young girl, my mother walked a lot. It was a cure-all, along with oysters stewed in milk and draughts of black beer. Alone, and always safely, she explored pathways and ginnels. Her favourite walk to 'Sugarwell' was reached by crossing Chapeltown Road, taking the road past the Recreation Ground, going down Buslingthorpe Lane, and thence via Scott Wood Lane to the top. She might just have caught sight of Scott Hall, a Queen Anne mansion which had become encroached on by quarries, and sadly, demolished in 1900. My mother's walk can still be found today, but in the lower parts it has become a narrow, muddy, rather sinister-looking path. Along the bottom there was another little lane, Low Wood Lane, also reduced to a track between hedges that were once were, and one or two wrecked cars have to be stepped around. A better way to see the old windmill (now converted into a private dwelling) is by way of a made up path crossing the rise just beside the entrance to the Meanwood Valley Urban Farm. Mother would have enjoyed a fine sight from the hill, for the panoramic view of Leeds is astonishing. Binoculars come in very handy.

In my parents' day it was, of course, the duty and pleasure of many, to attend church or chapel every Sunday, though it was in order after morning service to stroll in Potternewton Park, where I made unremembered pram journeys. The young were guided by Sunday School, assisted by the Band of Hope preaching teetotalism, and by 'Giving Your Heart to God'. 'Have YOU given your heart to God?' the Superintendent demanded of my seven year old mother in 1893. 'Please, I gave it last year', she answered. This he accepted, although, as she told us in our childhood, he did not know that on the previous day of Saturday, she had taken part of her collection money and bought a penn'orth of Liquor Beans, but remembering the stern text 'Thou God See'st Me', had at once emptied them down a grate in Chapeltown Road. God, however, was merciful, he let her go to the Whitsuntide Treat.

At Whitsuntide, everyone used to watch out for children in their Whitsuntide clothes; girls paraded in white frocks, boys squeaked by in new boots. On Treat Day, scrubbed coal carts fitted with wooden benches waited to take the children to the country, which must have been rather nearer than it is now. Great dray horses stood patiently, coats brushed, brasses gleaming, tails plaited with straw. Every child was required to have on clean underwear and to show proof of regular attendance at Sunday School. As the carts lumbered off, a few poor stragglers hung about enviously, wishing they had gone to Sunday School instead of playing out in the streets, but perhaps their work weary parents lacked the spirit to make them go or, quite likely, the children had no Sunday best clothing to go in. Behind the coal carts came little donkey carts driven by the Hokey-Pokey man. Hokey-Pokey-penny-a-lump resembled very hard ice cream, and needed a good licking to melt it. Liquorice Ladders were an alternative, but these were not the favourites.

When the country field was reached, the children got down and were allowed to buy their sweets. Presently, the Superintendent climbed onto a chair and called for silence, and then 'Follow your teachers to the barn' he shouted. Mugs of milky tea were already in place at the trestle tables in the barn, and after Grace was said the teachers went round distributing food from big baskets, whilst keeping an eye open for the smuggling away of good things. Once more the Superintendent's voice was heard ...

No boy or girl may have more than one long buttered bun, one currant bun, one sponge bun, one piece of fruit cake, and two mugs of tea!

When at last the feast was over, games were played, unsuitably it might be thought, but there were prizes to be won. After this excitement, the tiring throng was marched to the Big House to meet the kind toffee manufacturer who had provided both field and tea. As a hymn of thanks was sung for him, he waved forward some servants who carried trays stacked with little tins of toffee, one tin for each child. When at last the rocking coal carts trundled homeward, many little souls fell asleep, and some cried because it was all over.[9]

Life for most continued comfortably and predictably in New Leeds. Little boys bowled iron hoops along quiet pavements, girls skipped and sometimes danced to the jangling tunes played on the barrel organ by the Tingerlary Man, whose little monkey Beppo, sat aloft wearing a blue jacket and a red fez. Father's boyhood delight was the Cavalry Barracks. Like many another lad he was taken to watch parades, and he got very excited about the shining brasses, the handsome horses and, especially the gleaming helmets which he could see rising and falling in time to the trot, as the splendid soldiers rode by, their legs encased in narrow trousers strapped down under polished boots.

After marrying my father at his beloved St Clement's on the 15 June 1915, mother was coaxed away from chapel and became a churchgoer (Figure 11). Many Cooper names were entered in the St Clement's register, mine included when I was baptised there. Sometimes my parents had tea with the then vicar and his wife, the Laidmans; and I have faint memories of my little mitt in somebody's hand as I toddled round the side of that soot black church to see Mr Laidman's hens and to be given a new, warm egg for next day's breakfast.

Although baptisms and marriages were performed at St Clement's, burials were carried out at St Matthew's, Chapel Allerton until 1915. St Matthews was affectionately called 'the old church' or 'Chapeltown church', as indeed it was, for it had been built for the convenience of the villagers; the Leeds parish church of St Peter's being rather too distant for their attendance. The names Chapeltown and Chapel

Figure 11. Harry Cooper and Mary Eliza Cooper shortly after their marriage in 1915. *Author's collection*

Allerton are really synonymous and refer to the same place - the town of the chapel. I doubt if my parents thought of themselves as being residents of Chapeltown, but of New Leeds. Today's 'Chapeltown' appears to cover what was New Leeds and the largish area around, although I think it does not include Chapel Allerton village. Old St Matthews was pulled down in 1935, but its tangled, tumbled graveyard remains, not far from the present Chapeltown library in Harrogate Road. The new church was built a little way up on the opposite side of the road. When we moved to Chapel Allerton at the start of the 1939 war, my father attended this church until he died.

Schools must be remembered. As well as the Buslingthorpe school mentioned, probably the largest Board School in New Leeds would have been the one in Cowper Street, still there, though now it has changed hands. My mother went to Thoresby High School, and my father to The Boys' Modern, which was then in Leeds, but new buildings which went up outside the city are now transformed into Lawnswood High School, a mixed comprehensive. For those who fancied commercial subjects, these were provided by Mr Hodgson at North Leeds Commercial School in Leopold Street.

Until perhaps the late 1890s there were few shops in New Leeds, as most householders had the advantage of home deliveries. Mama Dickinson had a regular cheese and butter merchant who called at the door, offering tastes of his produce on a little silver knife, before she made her choice. There was also a muffin man, going the rounds with a covered basket, ringing his bell in the winter teatime dusk. I believe that muffin men were around until the 1920s; and lamplighters too, taking their long poles to spark the gas lamps. Eventually, a parade of shops appeared on Chapeltown Road, set back from the highway. In my memory, I see a grocer, a greengrocer and fishmonger, a very noisy cobbler, and best of all, Miss Harvey's sweet shop, where she presided over glass towers filled with chocolate drops and other delights.

In an advertisement in a St Clement's music programme of 1911, Everingham the butcher had advertised cheerily:

> *If you cannot call then write, If you cannot write then phone. Either way, whichever suits you, or we will call at your home.*

As the daughter of a farmer who had also bought beasts for home slaughtering, Mama Dickinson knew about good and bad cuts of meat. Woe betide the child sent on an errand to buy hindlift who returned with inferior taildraft! Domestic help was then cheap, and all but the poorest families could afford at least a maid of all work, as with the Dickinson's Maggie, so many housewives had extra time for sewing and baking, and for jam and pickle making. Maggie, a country girl who could not read or write, was taught her letters by Mama. Helping to write out jam labels was a pleasant way of learning. All this, then, was the general look of New Leeds in its heyday.

But the 1914 war broke up the serenity of that sort of life, sweeping away so many young men, some of whom never returned to those comfortable houses in New Leeds. Earlier, some lads had gone off adventurously to the Boer War, the progress of that conflict being recorded by my father in his little books, with much excited comment such as 'Ladysmith Relieved!'. The 1914-18 affair, however, had a very different flavour. When at long last, the misery and horror were over, sad families tried to repair the broken strands of life, carrying on bravely with concerts and bazaars; seeking comfort in church or chapel affairs. Those whose boys had come home safely gave thanks to God, and perhaps as my mother did, they took another look through the letters sent home in those dark days, before putting them away, and keeping them; sometimes for ever.

Slowly, New Leeds slipped into change. The main road began to grow busier, making the city seem closer, although it was a good mile or more away. Thundering vans and lorries replaced horses and carts, which had often provided a daring ride for young boys who hung onto the backs. The more frequent trams swayed faster down hill to Sheepscar, passing John Wesley's broken nose. Away went the old Public Library on the corner, which, with the Police Station, had stood its time. The 'modern' building which replaced the library has now become The West Yorkshire Archive Service, and admission is of necessity, by, appointment. No more the open door which gave warmth to wandering characters. The benches outside on which they rested and lingered have been removed to make way for car parking. Entry to the building is gained by pressing a bell push on a locked door, and the premises of industrious Mr Derewonko opposite are long vanished.

Sometime in the 1950s the trams were replaced by buses, which speed recklessly into the city by way of Regent Street, no longer following the old tram route along North Street. We left New Leeds long ago, in the 1920s, but the older generations were content to stay in the homes they knew and loved. Through all the years away, my father took us on periodic visits to his mother at 'dear old number 3'. For old times' sake he chose for us to walk to West Park and catch a tram down to Wood Lane, where tennis courts and a stone wall once stood before the reign of the present Arndale Centre. Wood Lane took us along to Woodhouse Ridge, whose length we traversed until we could drop down into Meanwood Road and across to Buslingthorpe Lane, busy and odorous from its tanneries and leatherworks. The name Buslingthorpe seems rather obscure. *The Place Names of the West Riding* gives many spelling variations of Buslingthorpe, and mention has been made of the place as far back as 1258. There is an instance of one 'Buselin', though no person of the name has so far come to light in Leeds documents. We can read, however, that Buslingthorpe might once have had its origin in 'Buselin's outlying farm'.[7]

Over in Leopold Street, broken glass remained on the backyard walls, and Grannie's kitchen held its eternal carbolic air. The copper warming pan hung as usual on the wall, and the tea urn which had refreshed so many past gatherings still stood on the chenille tablecloth. In the drawer of that square table there was one of Grannie's mother's girlhood toys, a small box containing Victorian cut-out cardboard dolls on wooden stands, and all their coloured slip-on clothes of the period. When I was ten, I was given these, but, inevitably, the box and contents were thrown away in my adolescent years. Today, they would be treasures, and I mourn their loss. Unconforming Clifton was long gone to Australia, his attic sleeping quarters given over to fascinating lumber. One could poke about and find great grandmother's Quaker bonnet, or another, outlandish purple silk bonnet with long ribbons to tie; and great grandfather's old topper, furry and unbrushed in a leather hatbox, 'You mustn't try them on, they're precious' said Grannie.

On one of our visits to New Leeds, in the 1930s, we were taken to see two amazing sights. Scott Hall Road cutting through some of the old ways known to mother in her wanderings. Traffic could now run all the way to Moor Allerton!: And we saw the luxury *Paramount Cinema*, erected on the corner of Briggate and Lower Headrow, now today's *Odeon*.

Grannie was taken by Dick to live with his family in yet another tall, grim house, this time in Brandon Grove. Another generation of sons had grown up to live in this part of Leeds; two died there and another was lost in a bombing raid over Germany. Grannie Cooper died in 1943 among her precious magpie collection, in a neatly kept little room.

Immigrants of different nationalities have come and gone in Chapeltown Road. My mother taught Jews who had fled the Russian pogrom; many made their homes here, and a synagogue was built just behind Leopold Street. Most of the next generation of Jews moved to fairer suburbs of Leeds. In later years, Polish people came to Chapeltown, as well as Asians and West Indians, who set up a lively community there in an area which now extends well beyond what was once New Leeds. These inheritors will look from there to a newer Leeds in a fast expanding city; a dream of developers, just as New Leeds was so very many years ago.

Notes and References

1 Jackson R *Jackson's New Illustrated Guide to Leeds and Environs*, Leeds 1889 facsimile reprint Oak Hall Press, Burton Salmon Leeds 1990.
2 Family papers.
3 Stowell G *The History of Button Hill* Gollancz London 1929
4 Family oral history.
5 Family papers.
6 Family oral history.
7 Smith A H *The Place Names of the West Riding* part IV, p128 & 138

5. HUNSLET IN THE EIGHTEENTH CENTURY

by John Goodchild, M. Univ

ONE MIGHT REALISTICALLY ASK why the story of Hunslet in the eighteenth century should be of any more than purely parochial interest: why should a study of what is now considered to be a peculiarly pedestrian suburb of Leeds be in any way significant to a wider world? In reality, Hunslet's historical success was its ultimate undoing, and the series of pleasant hamlets interspersed with streams, ponds and large areas of common which were the Hunslet of 1800 were soon to accommodate the heavy workshop areas of the nineteenth century. When from the mid-twentieth century the heavy manufacturing industry collapsed, and it became desirable to remove nearly all the associated local housing too, what remained of Hunslet was very different from what had been there earlier.

But this study is concerned with the beginnings of industrialisation at Hunslet in the eighteenth century. Hunslet offered a combination of advantages to the technologically up-to-date capitalist of that period: it was an area of flat land, yet raised above the river flood levels and was well watered by two substantial streams. It had excellent import and export communications from 1700 when the Aire and Calder Navigation was opened to Leeds Bridge, and from c1758 when the surface of the road from Leeds to Wakefield was improved by a turnpike trust; it also possessed important raw materials in the shape of coal and clay - the latter utilised for brickmaking and for low quality pots. It had the added benefit of being owned by large numbers of relatively small area landowners, and of being within easy reach of the money markets, cloth markets and regional economic centre of Leeds, not to mention its fleshpots. But Hunslet, like numbers of other outer townships of Leeds, was in Leeds borough and parish, but hardly of it. From the seventeenth century it had its own chapel of ease, with the church ceremonies celebrated there or at Leeds parish church, and it was an independent township within the 1626-created Borough of Leeds, responsible for its own poor law administration, its own highways and its own system of township constables. Finally, Hunslet was a manor on its own, and its manorial jurisdiction so far as land tenure and transfer were concerned, survived far into the nineteenth century.

Although the maps of the eighteenth century show Hunslet as a series of hamlets, with some roadside development in Hunslet Lane, in fact its population at the first census in 1801, at one less than 5800 souls, exceeded that of several of the regional market towns, of Dewsbury, Pontefract, Wetherby and Barnsley for example. Hunslet approached in population the towns of Wakefield, Huddersfield or Halifax. It had indeed been in the previous century that the population of Hunslet had grown to such remarkable totals: it was during the eighteenth century that the advantages of transport facilities, adequate land, raw materials and a good site, had developed or, in some these cases, become recognised. In 1650, a Government inquiry, anxious for the good of souls, had reported some 200 families in Hunslet, while in 1743, during Archbishop Herring's visitation, the parson of Hunslet reported some 600 families in his township or chapelry. The Hunslet ratebook of 1763 records some 500 separate occupiers. At the first census of 1801, there were 1238 families occupying 1205 houses, plus 64 further unoccupied houses. These figures certainly demonstrate the growth in the numbers of families:

200 in 1650
600 in 1743
7-800 in 1764
1238 in 1801

Equally significantly and within shorter limits, the population of Hunslet had increased by nearly seventy per cent from some 3500 of 1775, to the 5799 of 1801. Some factor, or factors, were obviously at work which were causing Hunslet to be an employment magnet, and it is our concern to identify what these new openings were, and to briefly account for some of the social developments which occurred as a result of the employment changes. At the same time, we must bear in mind Hunslet's topographical situation in relation to Leeds; it was separated from that town by open fields, the last of which survived unbuilt upon until the mid-nineteenth century, and while looking to Leeds as a market for its goods, not being in any real way affected by its being part of the Borough of Leeds. The early Leeds Corporation minute books are conspicuous in regard to the history of Hunslet solely in making no reference to the place, although of course the mayor and aldermen did act as magistrates in cases criminal, which Hunslet was not without. Neither the trade directories nor the ratebooks of the eighteenth century give much detail in the way of occupations in Hunslet, to enable one to grasp something of the situation at the end of the century, at the culmination of the developments which we are to study. However the poll book of the great Yorkshire election of 1807 lists the names, occupations and political allegiances of 105 males, the owners of freehold property of at least forty shillings annual value, who took the trouble to go to York to utilise both (or only one, as they desired) of their two votes in the first contested County election which had been fought since 1742, when only forty-two voters had gone to York from Hunslet, itself an illustration of both the subsequent growth in population, and the continuing sub-division of property. The 105 males from Hunslet in 1807, less than four per cent of the total male population, probably constituted a goodly proportion of those eligible to vote, as there were but 139 owners of property (male and female) listed in the ratebook of 1788 (Figure 1). Their occupations in 1807 provide a somewhat random but not inconsequential cross section of local occupations. There were tradesmen typical of any community at that period which was largely self-supporting: joiner,

Figure 1. The first page of the Hunslet ratebook of February 1788.
John Goodchild Collection

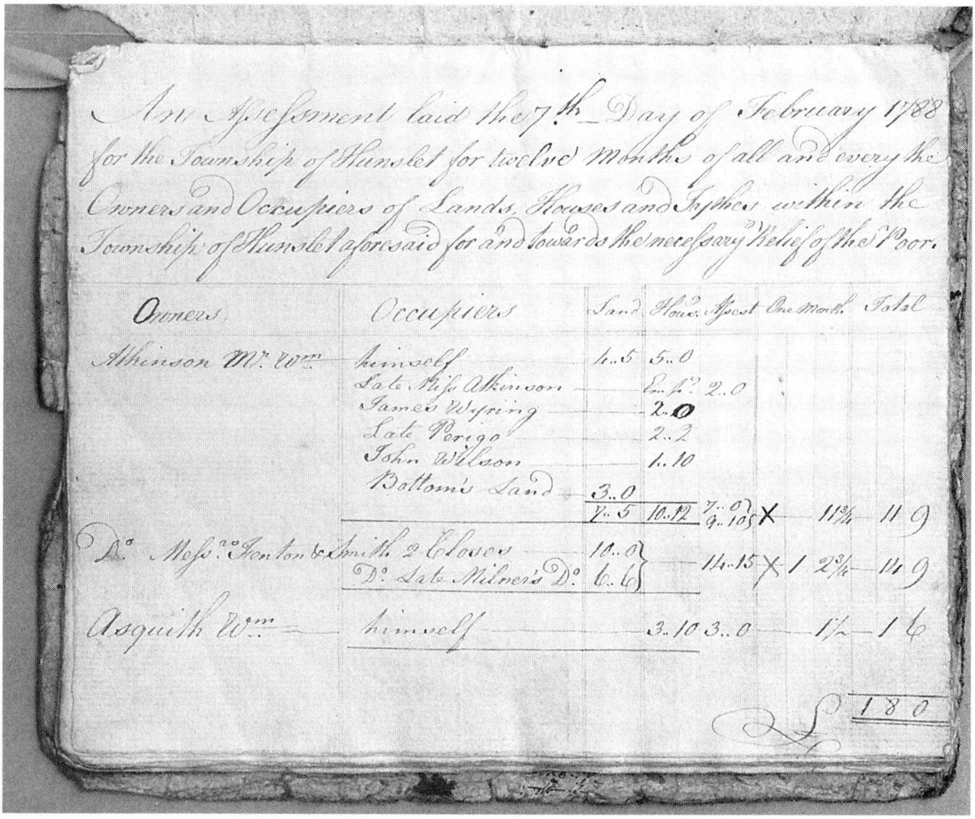

tailor, blacksmith and whitesmith, butcher, publican, ironmonger, shoemaker, hatmaker, but no lawyer or man of medicine. Then came the textile workers, with twelve handloom weavers, six cloth merchants and nine trades ancillary to clothmaking: dressing, fulling, scribbling, dyeing and cloth searching. There were four farmers and five maltsters and representatives of the newly established industries: potters, an ironfounder, wireworkers, glass manufacturer, vitriol maker, machine maker, and others who were in the construction industry of a growing place: four builders, a brickmaker and two stonemasons.

The first and essential change which had brought about this situation at the beginning of the nineteenth century, can be identified as something which had happened almost two hundred years earlier. In 1612-13 Sir Philip Carey, knight, had purchased from the Government of the impecunious James I, the Manor of Hunslet, its hall and its mills, with twenty nine-named tenancies, and extensive estates also in Liversedge and in other parts of the West Riding, for the very substantial sum of £4015 6s 7d. It is impossible to tell from the deed of conveyance if the sale was *de facto* of the whole of Hunslet, but quite possibly it was, and it was apparently also the area which the new purchaser, and indeed earlier his father, had tenanted of the Crown from 1572. Carey was hardly beloved of his tenants, who feared that he would increase their rents above those already paid, which they claimed to be the highest in Yorkshire. They offered to buy the Manor of Hunslet (alone) themselves, but were unsuccessful.

It is apparent from the surviving documentation that Carey and his son and heir John, then proceeded to sell off their Hunslet estate piecemeal; in 1621 for example, Sir Philip was selling two houses and two cottages; in 1644 the will of Alderman Beale of York refers to a debt of his of £600 still due for a purchase of Mr Carey, and in 1652 John Carey sold for £590 a house and land at Woodhouse Hill in Hunslet. Ralph Thoresby himself comments, of events in his father's remembrance, the younger Carey 'sold all the Lands, Mills and Wastes to the inhabitants' of Hunslet, although perhaps the two Thoresbys were not quite correct in their recollections. This newly-freehold population of Hunslet had at least a fair proportion of master handloom weavers in its numbers - the occurrence of the title clothier in the deeds of the period demonstrates the numerical significance of that occupation. But were the handloom weavers of Hunslet of such opulence as to allow them to build handsome and large new brick houses for themselves: one wonders if it was perhaps rather the successful cloth merchants of the town of Leeds who brought their successes to show in these new houses? Many were of brick, so would not date from before about 1610, and were probably somewhat later. Hunslet Hall itself, Carr Hall, Holmes Hall, one or two others with no known name, and some somewhat smaller old houses, survived into the nineteenth century. Puritanism flourished in Hunslet, as it did elsewhere in the West Riding among small freeholder handloom weavers and their neighbours, and a chapel of ease to Leeds church was built in 1629 and consecrated in 1636, with Presbyterian trustees who held twenty-four small annual rent charges of between eight shillings and fifty shillings each, to pay the minister; and documents show that collecting these rents was quite a headache. In 1636 the income of the trustees was £30 a year, which included £16 3s 4d from seat rents in the chapel. The chapel itself was of red brick, and was doubled in size, a significant necessity, in 1744 to sixty-nine feet long by twenty-seven feet wide, and by 1764 it had a bell, a clock, a stone font and a pewter basin. The parson of Hunslet, the perpetual curate in ecclesiastical terms, was appointed by the vicar of Leeds and, at least initially, the inhabitants. For some twenty-one years in the eighteenth century, from 1741 to his death in 1770 aged sixty-five, Hunslet was served by the Reverend Henry Crooke, and for nine of whose twenty-eight years his diaries survive. Crooke was the ideal eighteenth century clergyman: frequent in holding services in his chapel and in other houses, devoted to his parishioners, although quick tempered; he was willing to let his fellow-minister of the Church of England, John Wesley, preach in Hunslet Chapel in 1769 and stay in his home. He also held the living of Kippax, but paid a curate to do his duty there, and lived himself in Hunslet, where he also employed curates.

In 1743, the parson of Hunslet had claimed that of 'his' 600 families, 200 were dissenters, four persons were Roman Catholics, seven families were Quakers and the rest Presbyterians, presumably attending Mill Hill Chapel in Leeds or the slightly nearer Call Lane Chapel near Leeds Bridge. Certainly Hunslet mirrored the usual Whig adherence of the textile communities: in 1742, thirty-three of the forty-two voters voted Whig, and in 1807 fifty-one plumped for the Whig alone (there were also two Tory candidates) and nine for the Whig and the more moderate Tory, Wilberforce. By that time, Methodism in its various branches was widespread in Hunslet, and predominantly Tory in its politics. In 1754 the Independents had built their White Chapel in Hunslet Lane (later replaced by the present Salem Chapel), and close to where, in 1771, was built the

Leeds theatre. All were built between Leeds and Hunslet, and in the prosperous middle class residential area, as well as being easily accessible to the working class audiences. The Roman Catholics met at Middleton Hall and later at Stourton, immediately outside the boundary of Hunslet township.

Prominent in Hunslet's affairs civil and ecclesiastical were the Fenton family, in fact several closely related Fenton families. Numbers of the Fentons were in textile manufacture, but the senior branch of the family ultimately went into coalmining. Hunslet had had an ample and local supply of coal for its domestic, textile and trade needs from very local pits, but the opening of the new Aire and Calder Navigation in 1700 opened up entirely new, although distant, markets for local coal, while allowing coal produced downstream from Leeds to be brought by water to serve the town's growing needs too. The Fentons of Woodhouse Hill in Hunslet had taken large scale coal mines in the adjoining township of Rothwell Haigh by 1717, producing for more than local sales and utilising the new technology of the steam powered pumping engine. They were ultimately successful, with coal mining interests in Yorkshire, Derbyshire, Leicestershire and Nottinghamshire; interests in iron working, ropemaking, glass manufacture in Yorkshire and copper mining interests in Cornwall and copper smelting concerns in South Wales. In Hunslet, in 1739 Abraham Fenton opened a colliery with three working shafts, a steam pumping engine and a production of coal and maltmaking coke. He had previously worked coal on the Temple Newsam estate. A subsequent Fenton colliery worked in Hunslet from 1782 until closure in 1812, was part of the countrywide Fenton business empire; many of the Fentons were buried in Hunslet Chapel yard. From 1780 to 1795 the Aire and Calder Navigation worked a colliery in Hunslet, again with a steam engine, and close to their waterway; its accounts usefully survive.

What influenced Hunslet rather more, was the opening up of the Middleton colliery to coal sales in both Leeds and the Humber estuary via a waggonway system connecting the colliery's pits with both the town and the river, which appears to have been projected from about 1753. In that and the following year Charles Brandling purchased property in Hunslet, the township through which the connecting railways would have to pass, and in 1754 he bought a share in the Manor of Hunslet, across whose commons, vested in the Lords of the Manor, it would also be necessary to pass. Presumably the latter was the share in the manor advertised as for sale in 1752. In October 1753 Gilbert Cowper of Wantage in Berkshire, one of the

Figure 2. The only known illustrated letterhead of the Leeds Pottery in Hunslet used in 1827. *John Goodchild Collection*

Lords of the Manor of Hunslet, wrote that a person, to him then unknown, wished to take his share of the manor, and in the December of that year he wrote of a similarly unknown person who offered to be his tenant and preferred 'a greater Rent than any one Else. I suppose he Intends digging upon the Moor, or Comon'. Early in 1754 a Leeds attorney was apparently acting for a 'gentleman' in these negotiations with Cowper and reference is again made to the possible digging of the Moor, while in October 1754 the same gentleman wished 'to make free use of the Highways'.

The negotiations in regard to the crossing of Hunslet Moor, with its common rights and various Lords, and crossing the land of numerous other owners of land, were certainly being pursued on Brandling's behalf, so that presumably a railway into the southern suburbs of the town of Leeds, as well as another route to the river, was under active promotion. A real difficulty was found in regard to the latter in the form of the ownership of an estate which would have to be passed over in the making of a convenient route, being in the hands of James Fenton, who was already established as a major coalmaster who possessed easy access from his Aire-side pits to both the river and the town of Leeds, and who was obviously not anxious to accommodate a rival in both his town and downstream markets. Fenton refused to give his permission for Brandling's proposed line to the river to pass over his estate, and it was therefore necessary for Brandling to consider passing Fenton's estate on the public highway. As a consequence of a Sheriff's jury agreeing to this use of the road's surface in April 1755, the permission referring to 320 yards of Woodhouse Hill Lane in Hunslet, the waggonway was limited to a width of four feet and eight inches and other road users were to be able to continue to 'safely commodiously and conveniently travel and pass'. James Fenton and his Rothwell Haigh Colliery lessor, (the Duke of Norfolk) and Samuel Armitage Esquire appealed against the permission, but were unsuccessful. The documents relating to this case refer to permission to 'make and lay down with Timber Wood and other Materials a Waggon Way' of the length already mentioned. How long the railway took to build and when it was opened are unknown.

Meanwhile, negotiations were proceeding in regard to a railway route into Leeds itself. By January 1758 it was seen that short-term wayleave agreements with the numerous landowners on the proposed route were possible to negotiate, but that some of the sixty year lease periods which were considered desirable to warrant the necessary expenditure, were outside the powers of certain individuals to grant, owing to their tenures of the properties being for shorter periods. In consequence in January 1758 a petition from Brandling and 'others' was presented to Parliament, praying for powers through an Act for 'establishing Agreements' in such and other cases 'in order the better to supply the Town of Leeds with Coals'. In the same month Brandling had agreed in writing with several owners and occupiers (including the Lords of the Manor of Hunslet) to supply coal to Leeds at a fixed minimum price for a period of sixty years in return for permission to lay a waggonway, and the Parliamentary Bill received the Royal Assent on 9 June 1758.

Wayleave agreements were entered into between 7 March 1758 and 12 December 1759 with a total of fifteen owners of land in Hunslet and Leeds townships; all but two of these were dated before 17 October 1758. The wayleave rentals were modest, ranging from £1 10s 0d to £33 10s 0d a year, and some included land other than that required for the immediate purposes of the railway. Where the route was to pass over Hunslet Moor, the rentals were by acreage (8 an acre), as they were in one other case, that of Thomas Lee of Leeds. Some of the 1758 leases refer to the liberty being granted to lay 'Wood Timber Bricks Stone Earth Gravel Iron Rails Sleepers and other Materials' and most were for sixty years, the exceptions being single agreements for ten, thirteen, forty-seven (from 1771) and fifty years. Two of the original agreements survive in the writer's Collection while the whole were enrolled at the West Riding Registry of Deeds; certain of them refer to the new line being such 'as are commonly made use of for and about the Coalmines and Coal Works in the Counties of Durham and Northumberland'. Further land was of course required from time to time for the purpose of the colliery's transport undertaking, and in December 1787 Charles Brandling leased a piece of land fourteen feet wide giving access from the waggonway in Hunslet Lane to Meadow Lane, the term being for ten years and then as required, at twelve guineas a year. In 1809 negotiations were in hand for continuing the waggonway to the River Aire above Leeds Bridge, although Counsel's opinion, advising against laying the line, was taken.

So here is the Hunslet of the mid-eighteenth century, with its coal resources developing, although primarily for non-local use. The first development which was soon to grow into a highly successful venture may well have been the pottery, alongside the railway from Middleton Colliery which itself opened in 1758; the pottery quickly followed on Charles Brandling's land in the 1760s, with Richard Humble the able Middleton estate and colliery manager at one stage as its senior partner. It soon became, in Jack Lane, one of the largest and finest in quality of the potteries in England, with international markets and with some 150 workmen by 1789, while its success led to the establishment of other, would-be emulator potteries in Hunslet and Holbeck. By 1791 there were six pottery concerns in Hunslet alone.

Then came ironfounding. The foundry at Hunslet was worked from 1770, and by Salt and Gothard from 1772; another foundry was run by 1787 at Woodhouse Hill. Wire drawing and wire mesh working became something of a speciality of Hunslet and was flourishing by 1799. Malting was of some significance, and a brewery too existed by 1763. One Hunslet brewery was unsuccessfully advertised in 1797 and 1798, and its equipment sold off in 1798. A large chemical works was in existence in Jack Lane by 1791, run by Bowers & Co, members of which family were ultimately, and probably by about 1809, to go on successfully into glass making in Jack Lane. An iron rolling forge, worked by the water of the Aire, was worked by 1786; a paper mill with a steam engine existed by 1789.

But textiles continues to take their place alongside the newer manufacturers of pottery, glass and engineering products. Indeed, the mechanisation of the textiles processes and the adoption of power were very ancient in Hunslet; the power of the river Aire had apparently been harnessed by the twelfth century, and when Sir Philip Carey bought Hunslet Manor in 1612-13, Hunslet Mills consisted of one corn grinding mill and two fulling or cloth felting mills, and the story of those mills is subsequently well documented in the present writer's Collection. It is important to remember that for hundreds of years, the highest rateable value in Hunslet was the value of the Hunslet Mills; there were similar corn and cloth fulling mills upstream at Leeds and downstream at Thwaite and Fleet, and Hunslet Low or Knostrop Mills were possibly built in 1743.

The new technologies of the second half of the eighteenth century were soon taken up by opportunist entrepreneurs; this applied to textile technologies as much as to any other manufacture. In the 1780s the first powered raw wool processing machinery was introduced into the West Riding, and it was apparently in 1787 that two textile mills were opened in Hunslet. One was built by William Copley, close to the Wakefield turnpike, on the Balme Beck side. Copley had hitherto been a master handloom weaver, and quite an amount of documentation survives in relation to his mill, although he was unsuccessful. In 1787 also, the Stoney family, who by 1781 had built an oil crushing mill on land they bought in 1776, built a cotton spinning mill alongside the Balme Beck, at the back of Hunslet Chapel: Waterloo Mill as it was called, obviously at a later date. In 1786 three woollen scribbling machines and a wool willey had been advertised for sale by the Stoneys, perhaps worked by a horse engine of the kind which is known to have existed at Hunslet Moor side in 1805, powering a small cotton mill. But the larger of the new mills of 1787 were steam powered, utilising the then not uncommon (because it was both compact and inexpensive) Savery type engine, which in effect sucked up water to power a waterwheel; the Balme Beck was insufficient in its flow to provide water power itself. Further woollen and cotton spinning mills were built in Hunslet during the 1790s, probably five of them. Fire was to destroy a number of these.

It will be noted that Hunslet used all the forms of power then popular; water, wind (at the Leeds Pottery flint mill), steam reciprocating (Newcomen) and steam water-raising (Savery), with horse power too. Later both Boulton & Watt and Murray (high pressure) engines were also to be used here for power provision.

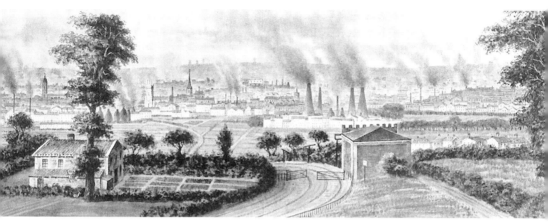

Figure 3. A view over Hunslet in about 1840. *John Goodchild collection*

Agriculture remained a recognisable Hunslet industry, even to the extent that horse gates and horse pasturing were still allocated on Hunslet Common, while the farmers of Hunslet voting in 1807 have already been alluded to. As late as 1817 some seven per cent of Hunslet's titheable land grew barley and oats, and some five per cent wheat and peas, with arable fields remaining to be shown in Hunslet and between Hunslet and Leeds in the six inch Ordnance Survey sheet surveyed in 1846-47, although those had gone by the time of the next Ordnance Survey issue in the 1890s. The common land of Hunslet remained unenclosed, and the Manor of Hunslet continued a significant entity, with surviving documentation up to 1890 and still administering copyhold property into the nineteenth century (Figure 3).

The road from Leeds to Hunslet, partly in each of those townships and only from 1758 a turnpike, was to be one of the earliest major ribbon development areas outside the urban centre of Leeds itself. The fine house, the *Black Bull* in Hunslet Lane which was only wantonly destroyed in our own time, had a house on the site by 1683 and subsequently members of the Kitchingman family, merchants and mayors of Leeds, lived there. When sold in 1726 there were stables, merchant's workshop, garden and orchard and garden house, when all was sold for a substantial £1110 10s 0d, and the title deeds of other of these houses show that they were substantial mansions indeed, but each had its workshops and warehouses for cloth finishing and storage. The Hunslet ratebook of 1763 demonstrates that there were then no major dominant landowners in Hunslet, but it shows several large houses in Hunslet Lane with substantial rateable values and owned or occupied by men described as 'Mr' and in one case, that of Anthony Cook, even as 'esquire', even though there were properties rated more highly than his. The 1798 trade directory lists some thirteen cloth merchants living and working from houses in Hunslet Lane (and others may have been partners and retired merchants), together with three woolstaplers. Some of these big houses were owned by the immigrant cloth merchants of the early eighteenth century, the Busks, Noguiers and Berkenhouts. Only early in the nineteenth century did these houses begin to slip socially, as their inhabitants were dispersed through natural causes, and one family at least, the Hainsworths, moved to the new Park Place in west Leeds, a newly fashionable area.

In Hunslet itself were, as we have seen, a number of fine seventeenth century brick houses, mansions, interspersed in an *ad hoc* manner with more humble homes. In connection with both occur references to tenters and dye leads, attributes of cloth manufacturing, and nearby were of course the two Leeds cloth halls at which cloth could be sold to the merchants, if not initially specifically ordered by the merchant. For the less affluent, rows of cottages were increasingly built. In 1763 apparently only one block of as many as four cottages existed in Hunslet, but by 1788 there were two rows of ten cottages, one of eleven, and one each of eight, six and five cottages. The more far-sighted, and perhaps the more financially able of the working population, took advantage of friendly societies to insure against accident, unemployment, old age and death, and by 1803 there were two friendly societies in Hunslet, with some 400 members in all. There was also the Hunslet Humane Society for the benefit of the poor, which existed in 1795. For the unfortunate who did not or could not self-insure, a Hunslet workhouse was opened in 1761. The township's civil vestry minutes survive from 1760 and as usual, the costs of maintaining the poor rose as the century advanced. In 1776 the cost was some £350, in the mid 1780s some £460 and by 1803 a huge £2220. In 1803 the rates were standing at 10s 6d in the pound; there were then in Hunslet thirty-nine residents in the workhouse and a further 120 adults receiving permanent assistance in out relief, plus 139 children; 240 more received occasional relief. Thus approaching ten per cent of the total population of 1801 were in receipt of some degree of poor rate funded relief.

Hunslet was able to provide its own schooling facilities. Alderman William Massie, an alderman and mayor of Leeds in the later 1680s, who died in 1699, left the capital of £100 for the benefit of educating poor Hunslet children, and by his will of 1730 the parson of Hunslet left a further fifty shillings a year to pay for the education of a further five poor children, who were to be nominated by his successors; the parents of the rest had to pay. In 1795 Hunslet advertised for a new schoolmaster.

So although the appearance of the Hunslet of 1800 was still predominantly rural, even at visual level the smoking potteries, kilns and the chimneys of the textile mills, ironworks, paperworks, chemical works and collieries were newly evident, visual innovations of the last four decades at the most, and the glassworks had certainly also risen above the level of the houses soon after 1800, and of course the world's first successful steam locomotives came across Hunslet Moor in 1812. The Hunslet of 1800 was changing, growing in population and growing in the number and size of its manufacturers. It was ready to become one of the great nineteenth century workshops of the world.

A note on Sources

All the information used in this article are to be found in the John Goodchild Collection, The Local History Study Centre, Drury Lane, Wakefield.

6. POOR BUT HAPPY: HOLBECK IN THE THIRTIES

by Ray Dobson

I WAS BORN IN LEEDS IN 1929, an only child. My father was born in Holbeck, in December 1900; my mother was born two years later, and lived in Glasshoughton, near Pontefract. When her father was killed in an accident in the pit, her mother, who had six children, eventually remarried and moved to Lower Wortley in Leeds. My parents met in 1924, when dad was playing in a semi-professional dance band called the *Cincinnati Players* (Figures 1 & 2). They married in 1928.

In the 1930s and early forties, Holbeck, although an area of Leeds, was a tightly knit community of artisan families. The lowly paid workers lived in rented, soot festooned back to back terrace houses with shared outside toilets. Streets were cobbled and lit by gas street lamps. I think the average wage was between £2 and £3 per week. Very few married women had jobs. The men still had a Victorian attitude and insisted that wives stayed at home to look after the families. Financially the area was poor, but rich in communal spirit.

Figure 1. Cincinnati Players dance band. Harry Dobson standing next to pianist. *Author's collection*

Sections of the Dobson family lived in an area of Holbeck known as the Rydalls, which are still in existence. My aunt, mother's eldest sister, married to the brother of Councillor Herbert Blackah, lived nearby until 1932, when she moved to Kirkstall. Dad was born and died in Rydall Street.

Most of the Holbeck workers were employed in the local clothing factories, engineering works, and on the railways. Some worked in the pit at Middleton. Dad was a sheet metal worker, and I first remember him working at the Acme Engineering Company in Isle Lane off Balm Walk. Mother's chapel, Isle Lane Chapel, was adjacent to the factory. I clearly recall him getting another job at Jackson Boilers, two streets from our house, in Rydall Place. He was pleased with a weekly increase of four shillings in his wages, and membership of their superannuation scheme (Figure 3).

Friday was my favourite day of the week. It was wages day, and I got a penny spending money. Mum was very methodical and had a separate tin for each household bill. She had a secret way of supplementing the family income – membership of the Co-operative Society. Somehow, mum always produced a penny for my admission to what was known as the penny rush on Saturday morning at our local cinema in Bridge Road which had the prestigious name of the *Palladium*. Local people called it the *Bug Hutch*.

Figure 2. Mother at age 20 years c.1922.
Author's collection

In late 1937 mum took a part-time job in a local factory, destroyed later by German bombs. This meant my being in Grandma Dobson's care every morning. In these days of the late 1990s, my grandma would be called a child minder, but this is where any comparison with modern ideas ends. Although she was then in her mid-sixties she was a formidable person. She had been 'in service' as a young girl and was very hard. I had to earn my keep by doing a variety of tasks, which included errands – I once lost a florin (10p) in the snow.

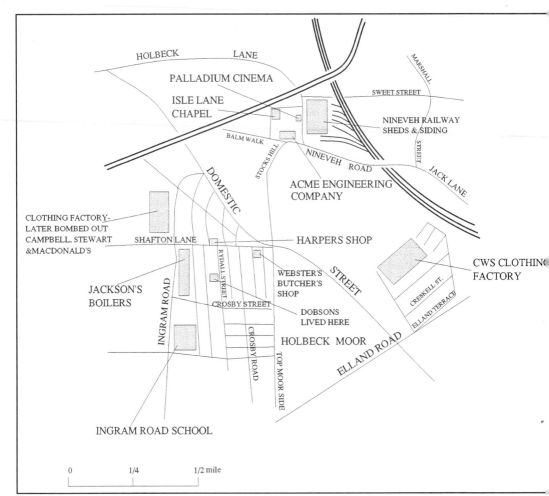

Figure 3. Map of Holbeck area. From Ordnance Survey 1906 1:2500. *Map redrawn by D Wycherley.*

I immediately felt the benefit of mum working. She started buying me the *Dandy* comic every week. The next year our annual holiday at Bridlington was extended to two weeks. My friends at school would not believe this. Although there were a number of pleasant occasions every year, our annual visit to Bridlington was the best (Figure 4). We went as a family. Our last family holiday at Bridlington was in August 1939. After war was declared, I would never have another childhood holiday.

A major change in my life happened early in 1942 when dad was taken seriously ill with kidney failure and nearly died. He was taken to St James hospital in Leeds, and then to Middleton near Ilkley. He was away for about three weeks. Due to the long journey out to Middleton mum could only go two or three times. Luckily, Auntie Annie, who had a car, went every other day (Figure 5). Mum must had done a lot of praying as her visits to chapel increased. Once again we were short of money. Grandma Dobson's discipline came in handy, and I did a lot of the household chores. To help our finances I got a Saturday morning job delivering groceries for a local grocer called Edwin Harper, who had a shop in Shafton Lane.

Harper, a miserable elderly man, had a Victorian master and slave attitude. Even though I was only a child he treated me like his other employees, and for the princely sum of 1/6d, I did two long journeys over hilly terrain pushing an old barrow loaded with wooden boxes of groceries. After the first delivery I was stiff and could hardly move a limb the next morning. Mum was upset and put me in a hot bath filled with salt. Soon I was back to normal.

After the first two or three weeks I got quicker and found some short cuts. This meant I was getting back to Harper's shop before my finishing time of one o'clock. Instead of letting me go home, he then sent me down into the cellar to chop up butter barrels for firewood, which he sold to his customers. Mum did not like this, and had me calling in at home for a cup of tea, before returning to the shop six or seven minutes before one o'clock. He never said anything. Perhaps the fact that he feared Grandma Dobson greatly may have had something to do with his silence.

My childhood officially ended in March 1943. I had attained the school leaving age of fourteen years. It was the end of a happy period in my life, and the start of the growing up process. In the middle of

Figure 4. Family Group at Bridlington in August 1930. *Back row:* (left to right), Uncle Archie Blackah, Grandad Dobson. *Front row:* (left to right) Cousin Irene, Auntie Annie Blackah, Auntie Elsie, Mother (holding baby Ray), Grandma Dobson, Dad. *Author's collection*

Figure 5. Auntie Annie, with cousins, Irene and Ivy. The baby is the author c. 1930. *Author's collection*

1990 I returned to Holbeck to attend a reunion at my old school in Ingram Road, before it was demolished. The ravages of time had been unkind to some of my former school friends.

Pure nostalgia had tempted me to go earlier for a tour round the streets I had known as a child. Many of the back to back houses were still there, but all the street cobbles and the gas lit street lamps had gone. Many of the houses were sporting modern dormers. All, or most of the outside toilets had been pulled down or the yards bricked up (Figure 6). The empty streets we had played in, under the old gas lamps, were now full of cars. There were mainly ethnic minority children playing, but did not seem as carefree as we had been. On the other hand, perhaps I was looking at them through the eyes of an elderly man. Holbeck Moor looked the same, apart from the fact that the old shale topping had been replaced with grass; a marked improvement. The moorside was unchanged. *The Britannia* and *Spotted Cow* public houses were intact. Holbeck Pitt Conservative Club, dad's only religion, was still there (Figures 7, 8 &9).

I was sad to learn that the once extremely active St Matthews church was no longer in use. It had been converted into a meeting place for the elderly residents of Holbeck. My favourite place, the *Palladium*, had been demolished many years earlier. I stood for a while just staring at the flat piece of land where I had enjoyed so many happy hours as a child.

The number 101245 had been etched on my mind for the best part of sixty years. Mother's little black book with this number boldly

Figure 6. Holbeck Street in 1990 – note old toilet yard still intact. *Author's collection*

displayed on the front was her Co-operative membership and dividend shares reference. Mother always made me go to the Co-op in Elland Road for odd items. My round trip of almost half a mile took me past chain store shops of the time, such as Thrift Stores and Gallons, together with other large shops. Sometimes I went for a single article such as a jar of jam or a bag of tea. My pleas about there being nearer shops went unheeded. Sometimes she would say it was the 'divvy'. She never realised that I did not understand, but being a Methodist, giving a truthful answer made her happy. I was about ten years old, when I learned purely by accident, the real secret of the six digit number.

It was a twist of fate that one day we were sent home from school due to a boiler breakdown. I can still see the perplexed look on her face as I explained the situation. I know there was something special afoot, as she was in her Sunday best, and wearing the special occasions hat with a veil. 'There's nothing else for it,' she said, 'You'll have to come with me' (Figure 10).

Some fifteen minutes later we were on a number eleven tramcar heading for the middle of Leeds. Mother was like some broody salmon heading for the spawning grounds. During the twenty minute journey she hardly spoke, but kept looking at her Co-op book with the number 101245 on the front. I sighed with relief: we weren't going to a Methodist prayer meeting.

It was only a short distance to the large collection of city centre

Figure 7. *The Britannia* Public House, Moorside, Holbeck c. 1990. *Author's collection*

buildings in Albion Street, These impressive buildings were the flagship of the Leeds Co-operative movement, and housed a wide variety of shops and offices. It was known to everybody as the LICS (Leeds Industrial Co-operative Society). Every man there seemed to be dressed in a dark suit, with a white shirt and bow tie.

Where we lived, men only dressed like this for funerals. Mum and I were directed to a very large room, known as the Peoples Hall. Orderly queues of mainly women filled the place, and everyone

Figure 8. *Spotted Cow Inn*, Moorside Holbeck c.1990. *Author's collection*

Figure 9. *Holbeck Pitt Club,* Shafton Lane, Holbeck, c. 1990. *Author's collection*

seemed to be talking at the same time. Whenever I see a group of women in one place I always recall this scene.

The numbers in our queue slowly reduced, and eventually we arrived in front of a dark suited man seated behind a large tressle table. I shuddered slightly as he looked a bit like our headmaster. 'Number please', he snapped curtly. Mother straightened up to her full height with a proud look on her face. '101245', she replied and handed over her precious book. He ran his ruler down his page 'Ah, here we are Mrs Dobson. The divvy is 12.5% this year.' Mum's face beamed, even though she did not know what he meant. 'Sounds good', she responded, hoping she had said the right thing. He pressed some keys on a box and pulled a handle. A small length of paper appeared, and he tore it off. 'Mrs

Figure 10. Mother at age 32 years, c. 1934. *Author's collection*

Dobson, your divvy this time amounts to £8 11s 9d'. Her hands shook as he counted out the money. 'Thanks for being a good customer, and I'll see you next year.' Little did he know that in a few week's time we would be involved in a war with Germany.

Mother had received the equivalent of four weeks wages. She was so pleased that she took me into the posh café on the first floor. Our previous visits to a café had been Sam's snack bar outside the bus station, where I usually got a mug of tea and a piece of toast. This time, I fed regally on a large portion of boiled ham and chips, together with buttered bread cut in triangles. We even had our own teapot and a jug of hot water. Throughout the meal mum could not stop talking about her windfall. I was more interested in the cubed sugar which I had not seen before.

The LICS was a wonderful organisation for working people. Food standards were good, and the assistants well trained. Pre-packed foods were years away. Almost without exception, every item was weighed out and bagged by the serving assistant. Most granulated foods were kept in bins, jars or boxes. Biscuits were usually in glass fronted tins, and would be mixed by the assistant, if requested, during weighing out. Each large shop manager had the same status as a bank manager. One of this elite band lived near us, and everyone treated him with great respect. In the lean years between the wars, the Co-op must have been a boon to women folk running a home on one wage, or the dole.

Whilst going through mother's personal things after her death, I discovered an old leather bag. It was full of old Co-op bills for a wide variety of goods including my Whitsuntide clothes. Also there was an instalment payment book for a new piano from Archibald Ramsdens in Leeds which cost £59 15s 0d plus interest (Figure 11). This reminded me of my piano teacher, Violet Craven. She was anything but a violet, being a ruthless taskmistress with a penchant for rapping young knuckles with a ruler. Mother's dividends over the years totalled almost £126, a fortune in those days. No wonder she had me doing half-mile errands. For a few seconds I felt humble and close to tears.

In the heyday of the Co-operative movement, there were approximately 5000 shops, and 100 superstores in the north. Had this mighty organisation progressed with the times they could have easily have competed with the present day supermarkets. To cope with changing times, the LICS complex in Albion Street has undergone major changes. Yet, even now, when I go shopping there, odd traces of the old shop atmosphere still linger. This could of

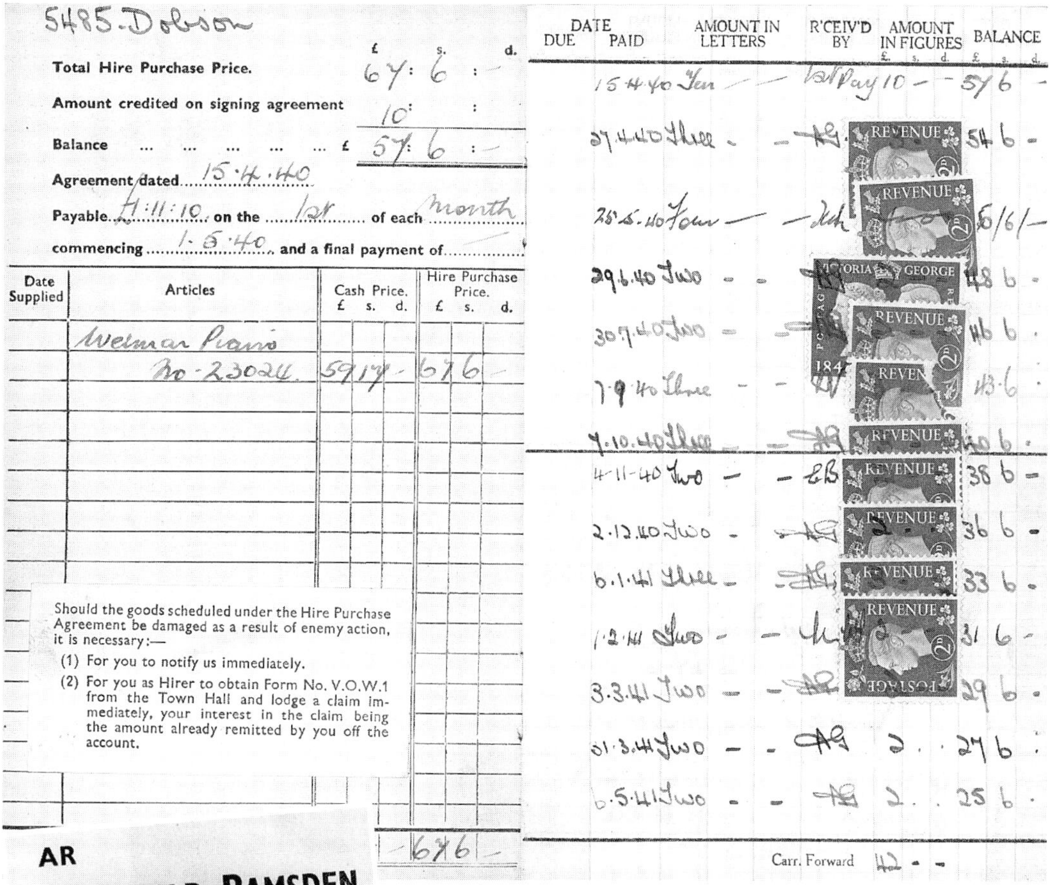

5485 Dobson

	£	s.	d.
Total Hire Purchase Price.	67	6	–
Amount credited on signing agreement	10		
Balance ... ... £	57	6	–

Agreement dated 15.4.40

Payable 4 : 11 : 10 on the 1st of each month

commencing 1.5.40 and a final payment of

Date Supplied	Articles	Cash Price. £ s. d.	Hire Purchase Price. £ s. d.
	Welmar Piano		
	No - 23024.	59 17 -	67 6 -
			67 6 -

Should the goods scheduled under the Hire Purchase Agreement be damaged as a result of enemy action, it is necessary:—

(1) For you to notify us immediately.

(2) For you as Hirer to obtain Form No. V.O.W.1 from the Town Hall and lodge a claim immediately, your interest in the claim being the amount already remitted by you off the account.

DATE DUE	DATE PAID	AMOUNT IN LETTERS	R'CEIV'D BY	AMOUNT IN FIGURES £ s. d.	BALANCE £ s. d.
	15.4.40	Ten		10 – –	57 6 –
	27.4.40	Three			54 6 –
	25.5.40	Four			50 6 –
	29.6.40	Two			48 6 –
	30.7.40	Two			46 6 –
	7.9.40	Three			43 6 –
	7.10.40	Three			40 6 –
	4.11.40	Two	EB		38 6 –
	2.12.40	Two		2 – –	36 6 –
	6.1.41	Three			33 6 –
	1.2.41	Two			31 6 –
	3.3.41	Two			29 6 –
	31.3.41	Two		2 – –	27 6 –
	6.5.41	Two		2 – –	25 6 –

Carr. Forward

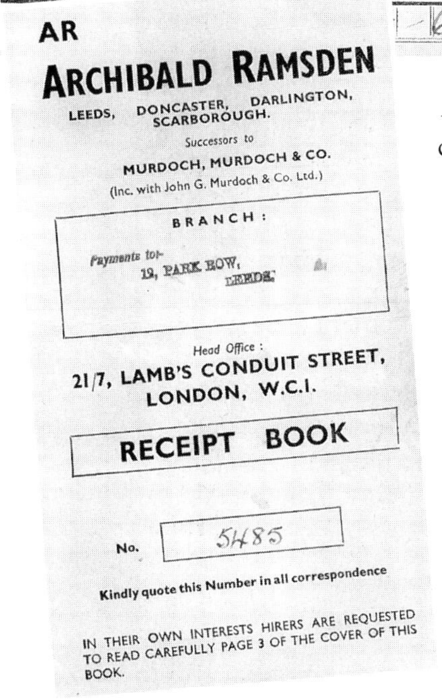

AR

ARCHIBALD RAMSDEN

LEEDS, DONCASTER, DARLINGTON, SCARBOROUGH.

Successors to

MURDOCH, MURDOCH & CO.

(Inc. with John G. Murdoch & Co. Ltd.)

BRANCH:

Payments to:- 12, PARK ROW, LEEDS.

Head Office:

21/7, LAMB'S CONDUIT STREET, LONDON, W.C.1.

RECEIPT BOOK

No. 5485

Kindly quote this Number in all correspondence

IN THEIR OWN INTERESTS HIRERS ARE REQUESTED TO READ CAREFULLY PAGE 3 OF THE COVER OF THIS BOOK.

Figure 11. Archibald Ramsden's payment card.
Author's collection

course be pure nostalgia.

Often, I still picture mother proudly collecting her divvy, and that small boy learning the secret of the magic number. Her diligence was for the benefit of her family. She herself, must have trekked untold miles to earn that precious dividend money. Who knows, maybe once a year her ghost visits Albion Street. In life, she was not only a Methodist, but member 101245 of the LICS. Yes, my dear mother had two religions.

In January 1938, when I was almost nine years old, it was necessary for mother to take a job. Whilst in Grandma Dobson's care I used to do a number of jobs. Whilst showing my granddaughter Emma an old two shilling piece, which was then known as a florin, I remembered an ill fated errand involving this type of coin (Figure 12).

I can still see that Tuesday morning. Snow was falling heavily like large pieces of cotton wool from an almost black sky. A strong wind was driving the snow into deep drifts on exposed corners. The conditions were no good for running errands. In a way, I was pleased that it was such bad weather. I felt certain that even grandma would not send me out on errands, but it was not to be, and decided that she wanted some stewing meat and offal for her pets. She handed me a florin (10p) with instructions to go to Webster's butcher's shop in Shafton Lane. My pleas about getting wet fell on deaf ears. In those days, small children did not argue with older people. Mother told me that I had to obey her instructions, as we could not afford to upset her. Mother's job depended on my being in her care before going to school. After plodding through deep snow, I was about 100 yards away from Webster's shop when it happened. There was a hidden patch of ice, and my feet went from under me. Whilst I was airborne, the silver coin flew from my grasp into the snow. The trouble was, that I never saw where it landed, though I knew roughly the direction in which it had travelled.

I got up and brushed the snow off my clothes. Then I set about feeling in the snow for the missing coin. Anxiously I reached further into the snow scooping out large handfuls. After about five minutes, my hands were blue with cold, and I gave up the search. Thoughts of Grandma Dobson made me shiver all the more. 'You stupid boy,' she screamed. 'Get back and find it.' She shook me severely. 'Don't dare come back until you've found it.' I screamed back. 'I can't grandma. It's time for school. If I'm late I'll be in serious trouble.' Tears were running down my cheeks. 'Well then young man, you'll have to tell your teacher that you've got to find my money.' She ignored my tears and pushed me out of the door. 'Don't be long,' she snorted.

Every laboured step to Ingram Road school was taking me nearer

Figure 12. Author at 8 years, c.1937.

to our feared teacher Mr Oakes. A man famous for his instant judgement and use of his cane called 'Laurie'. At the very least I could expect 1000 lines, which would have to be done in detention outside school hours. Mr Oakes listened to my tale of woe with a stony like look on his face . His face hardened wh en I told him that I had to go back and look for the missing florin. Chills were running up and down my spine, and there was an eerie silence as thirty seated pupils listened to every word. 'Is that the end of the story, Dobson?' He enquired sharply. 'Yes... yes sir. I've told everything, and I'm sorry - really sorry. It was just an accident in the snow.' After sitting quietly, he jumped up from the chair. 'You stay here boy. I'm going to see the headmaster, Mr Phipps. The rest of, get on with your work. Any trouble, and some of you will be shaking hands with Laurie'. The class were mumbling during his absence discussing my fate. I did not fancy a session with Laurie.

Mr Oakes made a quick return to the classroom. He pointed to the first row of desks. 'You boys and Dobson, come with me?' We were all ushered into the caretaker's store, and handed a variety of shovels and stiff brushes. Our small army, led by Mr Oakes and myself, made our way to the site of the lost coin. Fresh snow had all but covered my hand excavations. Between us, we cleared at least eight yards of pavement, examining each shovel of snow. In all we dug and swept for about two hours, but without success. It was a silent team that reported back to school.

Mr Phipps sent for me. He put his hand on my shoulder 'This is a silly situation Dobson. After all, it was a pure accident.' He paused. 'Don't worry boy, I'll go and talk to your grandma. She'll understand.' Some time later Mr Phipps sent for me. 'Sorry Dobson, but your grandma will not accept loss of the money. I'm going to discuss the matter with the staff at lunchtime. Whatever we decide, I intend writing to your mother about this unfortunate matter.' Ten minutes before the end of school Mr Phipps handed me a brown envelope. 'Please give this to your grandma, it contains two shillings collected from the staff. Also, give this white envelope to your mother. She needs to be advised.' A heated discussion must have taken place between my parents and Grandma Dobson. For the next two weeks I was looked after by Auntie Elsie. Dad sent a note of thanks and two shillings, back to Mr Phipps.

These days, a ten pence piece is a comparable unit to an old florin; but not in value. On 1938 values, a florin would be worth about two pounds today. It was a lot of money to an old lady, in the immediate pre-war days.

7. HIGH STREET AND QUARRY HILL

by Jane Greenwood

THERE IT STANDS IN ALL IT'S GLORY, Quarry House (affectionately known as the Kremlin); you either love it or hate it, the latest building to occupy Quarry Hill. It was built in 1993 as the headquarters for the Department of Health and Social Security; joining the *Leeds Playhouse* erected in 1990 (at a cost of £13.5 million). Now surrounded by car parks these two buildings occupy the whole of Quarry Hill (Figure 1). But have you ever wondered what was there before? 'Easy', you say 'Quarry Hill Flats'. Ah yes, Quarry Hill Flats, the vast complex that was built to house over 3,000 people. It was built by a system of steel and prefabricated blocks, it had lifts, an automated waste disposal system and operated its own incinerators to dispose of the waste. It had for recreation courtyards, playgrounds, kindergartens and nurseries, and it ran its own laundry, with dryers (an improvement on the old wash-houses); the height of modernity. But for all it's 'luxuries' many of the families that it was built to re-house did not take up residence there, they were happy to stay where they had been temporarily re-housed. These flats only remained habitable for forty years.[1] So, once again, what was there before.

It is possible Quarry Hill was the Roman site of Cambodunum; what is certain is that there were earthworks there. In 1645, during the plague outbreak, cabins were built on Quarry Hill to accommodate families who were suspected of having plague victims in their houses. Otherwise this area remained more or less uninhabited. Jeffreys Plan of Leeds in 1770 shows the old Methodist Meeting house and a few wayside buildings, possibly farms and houses of some size, but these were certainly not occupied by the wealthy as at that time they lived in the centre of Leeds.

Most of the area that today is occupied by Quarry House and the *Playhouse* was the site of a Methodist Meeting house, High Street and St Peter's Square; all of which had a long history of 150 years or more. The Quarry Hill area, until the late 1780s, had been somewhere for the inhabitants of the crowded Leeds to go and enjoy the waters, (waters that Ralph Thoresby himself mentions having sampled for their healing properties), the sport of bull baiting and generally enjoying themselves in the little time they had for recreation.

It was here on Quarry Hill in the 1780s that the East End of Leeds began its chequered history; it was one of the original sites of the infamous back-to-back houses. Union Street, Ebenezer Street and George Street seem to have been the only back-to-back houses before the ones on and around Quarry Hill. The houses on Quarry Hill were built by terminating building societies. These societies were formed by men of 'Moderate Means' who, on completion of the houses were able to rent them out to artisans and then realise a profit on the properties over a number of years.[2] Building Societies did not originate in Leeds, but in Birmingham, but their popularity soon spread.

Boggart Hill was a six acre field on the lower slopes of Quarry Hill owned by Lord Hawke, who had sold the site on which the Methodist Meeting house and burial ground now stood. On 6 October 1786 he sold the rest, five and a half acres, for £800 to two groups of trustees. These trustees were from two Building Clubs, the Boggart Hill Close Great Building Club, which would build St Peter's Square, and the Boggart Close Lesser Building Society, which would ultimately become the builders of High Street; the street which would stand until the 1930s, when it was pulled down to make way for Quarry Hill Flats.[3]

High Street was revolutionary in that it was built with the houses facing each other across a central road. Earlier house plots in Leeds seemed to have been built in a rather haphazard fashion. Here in High Street there were footpaths, called causeys, which were 4 foot

Figure 1. The New Leeds Playhouse and the DSS (know as 'The Kremlin') situated at what was the top of High Street.

6 inches (1.47m approximate) wide on each side of the street in front of the houses with a carriageway that was 19 foot 9 inches (6.02m approximate) wide. According to Jonathan Teal's drawing of 1790 there were two public pumps, 61 plots, of which 31 had been built on, and two public passages on each side of the street which led to the lanes running down the back of the properties. Originally these properties built by the building societies were to be two storey houses with doors and windows facing the street with a blank wall to the rear. As the houses were built up to the 'causey' there was plenty of room to the rear to erect another house backing onto the original

Figure 2. Map showing the layout of High Street, Quarry Hill and St Peter's Square before the clearance in the 1930's to make way for the Quarry Hills flats.

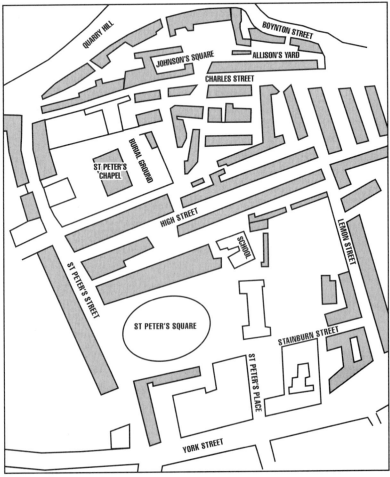

Redrawn from Ordnance Survey 1906 1:25000

one. Teal's plan shows some of the owners not only developed back-to-backs but had built further houses in the yards at the rear. The cramped conditions of the finished streets were already beginning to manifest themselves.

The Building Societies operated in such a way that the plots were not filled in order. Each new member paid a sum each week into a 'kitty'. The members had already chosen his plot or plots and, when enough money was available to build a house, lots were drawn to see which plot would be built on first. This continued until the street was complete. High Street took many years to complete and even after thirty years not all the plots had been filled.[4] Many plots were bought by speculators, some by owner occupiers who would occupy the house facing the street and rent out the house at the back and possibly the ones built in the yard. These plots on High Street had a ground floor area of approximately five and a half yards square (4.6m[2] approximate) with the possibility of separate cellar dwellings for tenants too poor to afford rent for an above ground 'cottage'.

Most of the original inhabitants, whether owners or occupiers were craftsmen, 22 of whom came from the building trade; 11 were employed in the textile trade; 16 were craftsmen, 5 were clerical workers, 2 had other properties, 4 worked in farming and 1 was a shop keeper! The street was unsewered and outside the range of piped water supply but, as has been mentioned earlier, there were two public pumps and No 55 happened to cover the site of one of the 'spa springs'. In later years No 55 would become the unlikely site of a Spa Bath House. There would be no industry near by High Street for another 30 years and the only public building being the non-conformist chapels. Eventually the East End would have corner shops, public houses and many of the properties would become notorious 'lodging houses' (Figure 2).

High Street was not without events of notoriety. The was the famous case of Mary Bateman, the Yorkshire Witch, who committed murder at a house on the corner of High Street and St Peter's Square. She was born Mary Harker in 1768 at Ainsby, near Thirsk, and is reputed to have shown early signs of a 'knavish and vicious' disposition.[5] She left home in 1780 to become a servant in Thirsk, moving from there to York in 1787 and then to Leeds in 1788, where in 1792 she married John Bateman, a Mantua maker, after a three week courtship. From then on she figured as 'a thief, witch and smooth tongued deceiver.'[6] Amongst her list of deceptions she passed herself off as a nurse from the Infirmary and played on the love-lorn girls and women of the area, offering fortune telling and charms for exorbitant fees. In time she ingratiated herself with two sisters by the name of Kitchen, who ran a linen drapers shop at the corner of High Street and St Peter's Square. In 1803 the first sister became ill after eating food prepared by Mary who also distributed medicine which she said she had got from a country doctor. The first sister died within a week, which brought her mother from Wakefield to the house in Leeds. She too was taken ill and like wise the other sister and by the time ten days had passed all three were dead. The local doctor was suspicious and inspected all the eating and cooking utensils in the house, but could prove nothing. He requested that the bodies of the ladies be exhumed, but there was no living relatives to sign the required forms so the matter was dropped. Mary had got away scot free. However, the next time she tried her 'poisoning act', she was caught. The intended victim this time was a Mr W Perigo and his wife. Mr Perigo lived but, unfortunately his wife died. An autopsy showed a quantity of arsenic in Mrs Perigo's body and Mary was arrested and tried in York. On 17 March 1808 she was sentenced to death, and hung the following Monday. Her body was given to the Leeds Infirmary for dissection and it was rumoured her skin was tanned and sold in small pieces to souvenir hunters; a grisly end for a terrible woman.[8]

Cholera came to Leeds in 1832 and was very virulent. The parish records show that from May to November 1831 there were 980 burials due to cholera. Some months later in 1832, 1,395 burials are registered. All together there were 1,115 cholera cases reported in Leeds; not all affected persons died, some mercifully survived. The outbreak was concentrated in the East End, of which High Street was a part. It was still not understood that the cause of cholera was infected drinking water, and this water in the East End was drawn from the river and streams that were contaminated by raw sewage and industrial waste. The drainage and sewerage imperfections of the East End street were considered to be the probable cause, though nothing much was done to improve them at the time. The East End was still classed as an unsanitary area in 1895![9]

The houses in High Street had fallen into a bad state of repair and in a report by Mr Baker, the Town Surgeon, in 1833, he stated that High Street had had seven cases of cholera which resulted in three deaths; the condition of the street was classed as 'generally dirty'. Lemon Street, which ran across the top half of High Street had eleven cases of cholera with five deaths, and its condition was 'a foot deep as usual.' Next door in St Peter's Square where the houses, which were not back-to-backs, were more select with small front gardens, there were seven cases of cholera with two deaths among the inhabitants. Conditions here were reported to be 'clean but confined'.[10] It must be remembered that High Street and St Peter's Square were Building Club street and were paved with roads made of setts; but all the Club streets were castigated for the low quality of paving, drainage, sewerage and water supply in the Sanitary Enquiries of 1839-42.

There were cellar dwelling in High Street and, by most contemporary accounts, they were horrendous places. These cellar dwellings were separate, one room dwellings underneath the back-to-back houses and were recorded as separate houses in the census of 1801. Whole families lived in a very small area, with only one window and door. The frontage was only five and a half to six yards wide (5m to 5.5m approximate). These cellar dwellings began to be cleared in 1873 but some were still occupied long after that date. A snatch of an old song of that time gives some indication of the plight of the people who inhabited these places:

> *Whe'ar all dahn in cellar-oil*
> *Wheer muck slahts on winders*
> *If we all keep us gobs shut*
> *Landlord ul niver find us*

There were some three-storey houses in High Street and some three-storey houses in St Peter's Square which had a lane running between them. Though St Peter's Square had pretensions of middle class housing they had windows which overlooked the back-to-back houses, courts and cellar dwellings of High Street and never achieved the middle-class expectations that the squares of the West End of Leeds did.

Originally High Street had no shop or public houses, but over the years houses were converted to accommodate such premises. One house at the corner of High Street and St Peter's Square was converted into a greengrocers before 1892. One of the most interesting houses on High Street became the High Street Spa (Spaw). it had been built on the site of one of the springs mentioned by Thoresby for their healing properties. It was No 4 (originally Plot 55) with its twin back-to-back. First of all it was known as St Peter's Sulphur Baths and was entered by the first passage on the right-hand side of High Street near St Peter's Square. The supply of spring water was by means of a 66 foot (20m approximate) deep well beneath the premises; and their were times when it was necessary for someone to descend the well to maintain the 'apparatus' which controlled the flow. A Hull firm of divers affected this operation by sending down a man in a diving suit. The bathing house mentioned in a Directory of 1847. A Mr Thomas Cordingly was the proprietor of the premises at this time and he advertised his establishment as having 'Turkish and Russian Baths alongside Sulpher and Spa'. Another tempting advertisement was for 'The Hot Bath House' which offered the luxury of 'Two towels and Flesh Brush for each bather'. After 1863 it was open from 7.00am to 9.00pm and catered for two classes; one at a shilling and one at sixpence. The last tenant was a Mr W Maude and the baths became known as 'Maude's Spa Water Baths.'[11] For many years an old portico stood in Back High Street marking the site of 'St Peter's Wells and Baths.' These baths were still in existence in 1908 but were cleared as part of the 'Insanitary Area'; the well was filled in and the baths themselves demolished by the Leeds Corporation who had begun slum clearance in the East End area in 1895.[12]

St Peter's Square already had some public buildings; it was the site of the General Eye and Ear Infirmary in 1812 and the Lying-in Hospital for Poor Married Women which opened in 1824. An isolation hospital for cholera victims was opened in 1832. All these hospitals were in converted houses and were not ideal as the Gas Works were situated in the next field. Industry was steadily closing in on the East End.[13] The Eye Hospital was opened for 'the gratuitous relief of the poor with diseases of the eyes'. Surgeons Mr William Hay and Mr Thomas Metcalf attended 'thrice weekly at 12 o'clock'. In the first month they treated 61 patients, 30 of whom were discharged as cured. These two surgeons had their own private practices and opened the clinic for the poor under a 'cloud of professional disapproval.' Originally this hospital was for outpatients only and it was many years before beds were introduced; but the poor were grateful for the services they received.[14]

Cholera was not the only epidemic to infect these street. Typhus fever raged in 1847, cholera again in 1848-9 followed by another outbreak of typhus in 1865-6. This last outbreak was blamed on the influx of Irish immigrants, but the condition that the street had deteriorated into must have added to the chances of those diseases spreading. There were other epidemics for the poor to deal with too, tuberculosis, typhoid and dysentery were among them. Improvements were made in medical provisions for the poor and these were funded by charities. The House of Recovery in Vicar Lane was closed and a new building in Beckett Street was opened in 1846 to deal with these diseases and a Fever Hospital at Seacroft was opened in 1893-1904 so taking the infections away into the 'country'.[15]

In an issue of the *Leeds Mercury* in July 1827 an event was reported which could have been serious for the residents of High Street; furnaces in a pipe maker's premises caused a subterranean fire due to the ignition of a small seam of coal just below the surface. Several yards of coal had to be cut out and the ensuing hole was filled with damp gravel.[16]

By 1882 the East End had deteriorated. High Street stood in the centre of a parish of 28,000 'densely crowded and dreadful houses'; these houses were in a long, narrow and dirty street. There was desperate poverty and in its midst was the local 'Muck Yard', used by the Corporation as a refuse tip; no wonder there were regular outbreaks of typhoid fever. Homes were infested with vermin of every kind. There were lodging houses of the 'lowest and worst types' and in a letter to the *Yorkshire Post* under the title *Condition of the Street in the Quarry Hill Area of Leeds*, the evils of furnished rooms, was pointed out in that immorality was openly practiced; that there was shameless 'Solicitation', and that gambling took place in the streets and open spaces. These conditions were not helped by the fact that there was inadequate light in the street and the courtyards. It was suggested that houses should be sub-let to respectable people, there should be more police supervision and more powerful lighting protected by wiremesh.[17]

Empty houses were allowed to fall into disrepair and High Street's reputation was very low. It was into this 'den of vice' that Mr T H M Brameld, an old boy of Leeds Grammar School came. He opened the Good Shepherd Mission Hall which was dedicated on Whit Sunday Eve 27 May 1882 and there were services on Wednesday 31 May, Thursday 1 June and on Trinity Sunday 4 June. When converting two houses on the corner of High Street and St Peter's Square to house the mission Mr Brameld was confronted with an infestation of vermin. For six weeks the building was stoved, but with little effect. For all of the 55 years Mr Brameld was involved with the mission the problem of vermin was never solved. These two converted 'cottages' were eventually pulled down and a new Mission Chapel and School were erected in 1891 and enlarged in 1894.

The Mission was originally opened for 'Young Fellows Morally and Criminally deprived'.[18] A survey of the Mission's district had shown that there were over 30 public houses; one street alone had eight and the average number of fights on a Saturday night were estimated at sixteen. The Mission held services on a Sunday and

Figure 3. The 'Good Shepherds' cricket team in the early 1920s. *Author's collection*

daily during the week. There were Sunday Schools for boys and girls and Bible Classes for men and women. One class was run by Canon Tupper-Carey and those who attended were known as 'Tuppers Burglars'! He had a great deal of influence over these young men and had very little trouble from them when they attended his classes. The Club House offered cricket, football, swimming and had a gymnasium; the young men went to seaside club camps whilst whist drives and dances were held for the inhabitants of the parish which must have seemed very civilised in these mean, deprived streets (Figure 3). In 1902 a Sunday school was opened for girls aged between 20 and 22. Here they were taught reading and writing in the hope of making them good church members. A Miss Juliana Baker set a good example for them all by opening a shop where all the profits went to 'God's Work Abroad'. The Mission remained open until the houses around it were demolished to make way for Quarry Hill Flats and left many happy memories for its members who had been given some hope in their desperate circumstances (Figure 4).[19]

The Mission fed the need of the inhabitants who followed the teaching of Church of England. Renovation of the Wesleyan Methodists St Peter's Street Chapel meant that they could accommodate 2,000 on a Sunday. There was always rivalry between the denominations and Walter Farquhar Hook, who was vicar of Leeds between 1837 and 1859 encouraged more involvement with the Church of England by providing school places for each child. He did this by splitting the larger parishes into smaller units; this in turn brought into being the building of more schools and churches. The Mission fulfilling the role of the church for the deprived area of Quarry Hill.[20]

The now growing Irish community, many of whom began to occupy the houses in this area used St Patrick's Chapel on York Road, which was built in 1831, but as the population grew a new Roman Catholic church was erected on Richmond Hill. Known as Mount St Mary's it had seating for 2,000. Not far down the road was the Central Synagogue which catered for the Jews who were also flowing into the area. All of these diverse societies lived cheek by jowl in desperate living conditions. In research into the 1891 Census conducted by Murray Freedman he found 24 households of Jewish immigrants in the High Street and St Peter's Square area; ten of which were single occupancies. This suggests that they were living in the notorious lodging houses in the area where, as the day workers left for their 'day's toil', their beds were filled by the workers returning from the night shifts.[21] How difficult it must have been for these people in a strange land and with a strange language to overcome.

In St Peter's Square were born two personalities who would have a link with those mean street through to the present day building on this site. The first was a man they called 'The Factory King'. His name was Richard Oastler and he was born in St Peter's Square in 1789 and his life and work connect from those times to the present. Richard Oastler was the youngest of eight children born to Robert Oastler who was a close friend of John Wesley. Robert Oastler's father disinherited his son on account of his Methodism. Richard was educated at the Moravian School at Fulneck in Pudsey and had aspirations of being an architect. He was articled to Charles Weston of Wakefield but weak sight made him abandon this work after four years.

Oastler became a Commission Agent, which made him a wealthy man, but he was to loose it all in 1820. He married Mary Tatham of Nottingham on 16 October 1816 and they had two children, both of whom died in infancy. Mary stood by him until her death in 1845. When Richard's father died he was offered an apprenticeship of Steward by Thomas Thornhill, absentee owner of Fixby. He earned a salary of £300 a year.

Richard had been an advocate of the Abolition of Slavery in the West Indies since 1807 and he supported Queen Caroline and opposed Catholic Emancipation. However his main concern became 'the evils of children's employment' especially in the Bradford Area. His letters to the newspapers, especially to the *Leeds Mercury* were many, but his article 'Yorkshire Slavery' was met with denial and criticism; but he exposed the truth of the conditions and earned the 'gratitude of the working man'. From these beginnings his involvement in the cause took him to London where he addressed meetings speaking in favour of the ten hour day and supported bills in Parliament with regard to this.

Because of this obsession with the working man's condition he left Thornhill's employ owing Thornhill the vast amount of £2,000. This was to involve him in a court case in July 1840 and by 9 December in that year he was committed to the Fleet Prison for three years. Undeterred, from there he published *Fleet Papers* pleading the cause of the factory workers. At this time he was also denouncing the New Poor Laws and defending the Corn Laws. His enthusiasm had great influence on public opinion.

Oastler was freed from Fleet Prison in 1844 after a Liberation Fund had been set up to pay his debt to Thornhill which, by this

Figure 4. Quarry Hill flats – the largest in Europe. *Courtesy of A Cockroft*

time, had escalated to £2,500. The fund fell short of this amount but the difference was made up by his friends. Sadness entered his life at this time when his wife died in Headingley in June 1845. He carried on the cause and published a newspaper called *The Home* from 1851 to 1855. Oastler died on 22 August 1861 in Harrogate but was brought back to be buried at Kirkstall where, in 1864 a stained glass window was dedicated to his memory in St Stephen's, Kirkstall. He was described as 'A Churchman, Tory and Protectionist, powerfully built, over six foot tall and had a commanding presence.' He must have been some adversary during his campaigns. The stained glass window was not his only commemoration. When Quarry Hill Flats were built one of the houses was named after him. He would have been flattered and now the Department of Health and Social Security stands on the site, with the possibility of the Benefits Agency to come. Could he have imagined in his wildest dreams that Government departments such as these would evolve to help his down trodden poor.[22]

On 3 March 1848 a little girl was born to an 'obscure actress named Brown', who was subsequently known as Mrs Bland, at number 35 St Peter's Square; the little girl, who was to follow in her

Figure 5. The DSS building in 1999. The back right hand corner of this building is sited where High Street and Lemon Street met.

mother's footsteps was called Elizabeth Ann Brown. Her true father's name was never revealed and Elizabeth Ann Brown is our second link with the present day. Her childhood was spent in the area before she went to Skipton. From there she went to work as a mill hand in Guiseley and then subsequently a nursemaid and a barmaid. She changed her name to Lizzie Ann Bland and went to London to chance her luck on the stage. Lizzie made her first appearance in Margate in 1864 in the role of 'Juliet'. She quickly went to London and in July 1865, at the *Royalty Theatre* in Dean Street, she played 'Juliet' again; it was a part that made her famous. She changed her name once more to Lilian Adelaide Lessont, which eventually became Lilian Adelaide Neilson, a name she kept even after marriage to Philip Henry Lee who was the son of the Rector of Stoke Bruerne near Towcester. The marriage did not last and they were divorced in 1877. John Ryder, an actor, took her under his wing and taught her all he knew. She travelled to the United States four times in 1872, 1874, 1876 and 1879 and is reputed to have had no English rival as a tragedian at this time. Strangely there has been little written about

Figure 6. The bottom of Eastgate 1999. This was previously the site of the old chapel and where Quarry Hill began.

Figure 7. All that's left of St Peter's Square today, a street sign.

her even though she is reputed to have been 'a remarkable beauty with a musically caressing voice, and girlish movements.' There is only one known portrait of her which is in private hands.[23]

On her return from America in 1879 she left for Paris. Her friends said that she seemed to know she would not return and she never did. She died there suddenly in 1880 with what was reported as some sort of gastric complaint. Her body was returned to England and she was buried in Brompton Cemetery.[24] When Quarry Hill Flats were built she too, like Oastler, had a house named after her, Neilson House. I wonder how many people living there ever knew the originator of the name? It is rather fitting that part of the site of Quarry Hill Flats is now taken up with the West Yorkshire Playhouse, the College of Music and the Yorkshire Dance Studios. (Figure 5 and 6)

By the 1930s High Street and St Peter's Square had been cleared away and the building of Quarry Hill Flats began; but High Street and St Peter's Square still presented problems to the modern builders in steel and concrete. The 'old cellars, gasometer bases, coal holes, culverts and disused burial grounds' were reported in the *Yorkshire Post* of 5 January 1938, to be causing 'difficulties'.[25] The old streets refused to die peacefully. Human bones were dug up as late as July 1953 but they were not thought important enough to cause great alarm. A hundred years earlier there would have been a hue and cry as this was the time when the parish church of St Peter's employed a watch over their burial ground because of the fear of body snatchers. The graves of the burial ground were desecrated in the name of progress when the railway line from Marsh Lane to Central Station cut across the heart of the community.

From the beginning of the century until the 1930s, the area covering High Street and St Peter's was slowly cleared; but as late as 1925 there were houses in High Street occupied by a greengrocer, a butcher, two general shopkeepers, a dairyman, a grocer and a florist.[26] What a long way from the 1780s to 1999 this small area of Leeds has come; from green fields noted for recreation to new housing for artisans, through the most ambitious modern housing scheme for the working man in the whole of 1930s Europe, to the services and recreations to suit the new century to come. (Figure 7)

Notes and References

1. Ravetz, *Model Estate* London 1974
2. Beresford MW *East End, West End: The Face of Leeds During Urbanisation 1684-1842* Thoresby Society Monograph LX and LXI 1988
3. *Ibid*
4. *Ibid*
5. Baines E *The Extraordinary Life and Character of Mary Bateman The Yorkshire Witch* Leeds, 1820
6. *Ibid*
7. *Ibid*
8. *Ibid*
9. *Ibid*
10. Baker R *Report to the Leeds Board of Health* Leeds 1833
11. *Thoresby Society LIV,* 1973
12. *Ibid*
13. Beresford MW *The Face of Leeds* University of Leeds
14. *Thoresby Society LIV*
15. Beresford MW *East End, West End*
16. *Leeds Mercury* July 1827 Leeds City Library
17. *Yorkshire Post* 1882, Leeds City Library
18. Leeds Parish Church *Good Shepherd Mission 1882- 1932* Leeds 1932
19. *Ibid*
20. Dalton HW *Walter Farquhar Hook, Vicar of Leeds: His Work for the Church and Town 1837-48,* Thoresby Society LXIII 1990
21. Freedman M *1891 Census Leeds, List of Jewish Residents*
22. *Dictionary of National Biography*
23. *Ibid Lilian Adelaid Neilson*
24. *Ibid*
25. *Yorkshire Post* 5 January 1938 Leeds City Libraries
26. *Kelly Directory 1925*, Leeds City Library

8. Colonel Harding and the Black Prince

by William Scott

EARLY IN 1902 Colonel Thomas Walter Harding DL JP, sometime Lord Mayor of the City of Leeds between 1898 and 1899 conceived a somewhat grandiose scheme which, he surmised, would suitably reflect the honour and prestige of his much loved City.

The demolition of the one hundred and thirty year old Coloured Cloth Hall and its famous rotunda thirteen years earlier had enabled a splendid Post Office to be constructed, but had left large areas of open space in what was to become the hub of the city and over which the city fathers had exercised their minds for some time. In 1897 work finally commenced on what was to be a famous landmark - City Square. It was completed two years later, a pleasant 'roundabout' surrounded by ornamental trees.

Colonel Harding, at that time fifty nine, had had a long and honourable association with Leeds. He had been a director of a well known local engineering company - Harding Richards Rhodes & Company, and in 1902 he became Chairman. He was also Chairman of the old West Riding Rivers Board and his military title was the result of seventeen years service with the West Riding Yorkshire Volunteer Artillery, whom he had joined when he was thirty six. He had command of the 1st Battalion for several years.

His service to the City had long been marked and his two year presidency of the Leeds Chamber of Commerce between 1889 and 1891 culminated in his election as Lord Mayor,which made him a familiar figure to the city's inhabitants. He wished to present his City with a mark of his esteem and one which would celebrate his sixtieth birthday; he decided to embellish and enhance City Square with an arrangement of statues.

During the remainder of 1902 and into 1903 Colonel Harding commissioned a number of sculptors to work on a setpeice of statues commemorating, where possible, famous local people. These with the exception of Watt and Harrison, were paid for out of his private purse (Figure 1). The centre piece of all this magnificence was to be an equestrian representation of the Black Prince in bronze. Why he chose the Black Prince remains something of a mystery as the only tenuous link the Black Prince has with Yorkshire, is the fact that the

Figure 1. City Square in 1903. The statues are those of Joseph Priestly, John Harrison, James Watt and Dean Hook. *Courtesy of the Leeds Civic Trust*

Prince's son, subsequently Richard II, was deposed in 1399 and was supposedly assassinated in Pontefract Castle.

Colonel Harding commissioned a well known Royal Academician, Thomas Brook, who was later knighted, to produce the statue. Brook decided to have the statue cast in Belgium. After several months work the completed statue was shipped from Antwerp in a huge wooden crate, measuring eighteen feet by eleven feet (5.5m by 3.35m). It was bound for Hull Docks where it was duly landed, on the west side of the then Humber Dock, late in August 1903. Due to the Colonel's association with Sir John Eaglesome, Managing Director of the Aire & Calder Navigation Company and to the fact that canal transport was smooth, efficient and cost effective, instructions were given to the Navigation Company to receive the statue and 'safely tranship and bring to Leeds by barge'.[1]

When the statue was despatched from Belgium, strict instructions were given that it had to be kept upright. However when it was shipped at Antwerp it was laid on its side on the deck of the steamer; and on arrival at Hull it was lifted ashore and similarly laid on the Quay. The Navigation's agent in Hull requested the Dock Authority to raise the case upright and lift it onto the awaiting barge. This the Dock management refused to do unless an indemnity was given them; as the Canal agent could not or would not accept that responsibility, Colonel Harding was contacted in Leeds and arrangements made for him to go to Hull on the following Monday, 24 August 1903.

In view of the delicacy of the operation, the Navigation's Engineer, Henry Pickard, went with him. The Colonel was most concerned during the journey to Hull, not so much from the financial implications of an accident happening but that if indeed one occurred, it would take a full twelve months to mould and cast a new statue and so hold back the completion of City Square.

On arrival at Humber Dock, the two men found the timber casing to be of substantial construction and so far as could be ascertained, well 'stayed' inside. In assessing the risks of lifting vertically, Henry Pickard took into account that the horse was only attached to the bronze base at three of its hoofs and that the strength at the fetlocks looked very weak. Deciding however that the designer would have taken into account the strain placed on the fetlocks by wind pressure when the statue was fixed in the elevated and exposed position it was to occupy, he advised Colonel Harding the lifting should go ahead and gave an indemnity to the Dock Authority for the use of their steam crane, with a caveat that the crane would only work under the

Figure 2. City Square 1903. *Courtesy of the Leeds Civic Trust*

direction of Mr Pickard. With a loud creaking noise the case was lifted upright, when it was discovered that in the side which had been laid on the Quay, was a large inspection manhole. Henry Pickard hurriedly scrambled inside and to his relief found everything satisfactory. It is recorded that the Colonel was invited inside also 'but declined'.[2]

The barge to be used was one of the Navigations' famous 'Fly' boats, which were fast, efficient and 'dumb' (that is not having its

Figure 3. The Black Prince by Thomas Brook RA - City Square 1903. *Courtesy of the Leeds Civic Trust*

own motive power but pulled by a steam tug). The case was lifted and lowered into the barge when the ever pernickety Colonel discovered that the head of the statue's Charger would be looking to the stern of the boat; he insisted that the case should be taken out and turned round. The phlegmatic Henry Pickard however, merely turned the barge round so that the statue was brought to Leeds with its head looking to its final resting place.

Whilst conscious of the honour bestowed, the two experienced tug crewmen treated the precious cargo as just another consignment and that afternoon steamed into the estuary bound for Leeds.

From Hull Docks to Goole the journey took just over five hours, the barge staying overnight in the Barge Quay there. Setting off next morning for the thirty three mile journey to the New Dock Basin (off Clarence Road) in Leeds, the barge train passed crowds of people who 'gave vent to loud cheers'.[3] The arrival at New Dock Basin on the morning of Thursday 27 August 1903 ensured a large crowd of curious onlookers. The Basin is still there, disguised now by much new building and the Royal Armouries. One of the dockside steam cranes was used to swing the crate onto the wharf, this time right side up, and preparations were made to move the statue. This was not as easy as first supposed. Whatever route was selected it was found that the statue would need to pass under a railway bridge but, after taking many measurements, the indefatigable Henry Pickard overcame the problem by obtaining the loan of a special low bogey, or boiler waggon. An important question was whether to have the bogey hauled by a traction engine or horse. In view of the subject of the statue it was finally agreed that only horses should be used. The case was lifted onto the bogey on the Saturday morning and delivered to City Square on the early morning of Monday 31 August in time for the citizens to see when they were arriving for work.

The *Yorkshire Post*, in its issue the following day commented:

In two or three days time the equestrian statue of the Black Prince will be placed in position in City Square, Leeds. The statue was removed from the barge which brought it from Hull yesterday morning; six horses being required to draw the bogey on which the heavy load was placed. A great crowd witnessed its arrival at City Square and when the case was opened and the fine figure of the horse was disclosed there was a murmur of admiration. The full merit of Mr. Brookes' work will not be seen until the charger has been placed on the pedestal and the upper part of the Black Prince has been bolted in its place. But the thousands of people who stopped to watch the operation of the workmen yesterday saw sufficient to convince them of the impressiveness of the statue and the artistic gain it brings the City.[4]

In recognition of the Aire & Calder Navigation's role the article continued

it is meet that the care exercised by the Aire & Calder Navigation in transporting the statue from Hull to Leeds should be acknowledged. The Officials gave the matter their personal attention and having delivered the valuable work without a scratch they have intimated to Colonel Harding that the Navigation wish to forgo their charges.

Two weeks later, on Wednesday 16 September 1903 and in the presence of over one hundred thousand people City Square was officially opened with the presentation to the City of the splendid statue of the Black Prince.(Fig. 2 & 3) Its benefactor, Colonel Harding, was accorded Leeds' highest honour and given the Freedom of the City.

Notes and References

1. Letter from Colonel Harding to Sir John Eaglesome.MD, Aire & Calder Navigation Company. Minutes, January 1903.
2. Henry Pickard.Engineer: A&CN Co. 'Reminiscences' *Aire & Calder Staff Magazine*, December 1928.
3. *ibid.*
4. *Yorkshire Post*,1 September 1903.

9. RELIGIOUS ROLES IN THE NINETEENTH CENTURY – SOCIAL GROWTH OF BRAMLEY

by Anthony Silson

The inhabitants of Stanningley, like those of Bramley...have been generally accounted the rudest and most unpolished in the district and their houses and their persons by no means exhibit any very remarkable attention to cleanliness.
(Edward Parsons, 1834)[1].

HAVING THUS DENOUNCED BRAMLEY, Parsons went on to admit there had been some recent improvement which he attributed to the Sunday Schools. However three years before Parsons wrote, Bramley's then perpetual curate, the Reverend T Furbank found people and houses generally to be clean but roadside channels to have filth and stagnant water.[2] If the people were dirty it was not without good reason, for water supplies and sewage disposal were grossly inadequate. And if the people were unpolished, with scant knowledge outside their trades and if some were petty criminals and vandals, it too was not without good reason for educational provision and the forces for law and order were deficient.

It was not until 1842 that Leeds Corporation obtained a *Leeds Improvement Act* but even then progress was delayed for many years in the town of Leeds, let alone Bramley, a frontier outpost of Leeds Borough, by an unwillingness to raise and spend money.[3] Trades Union members existed in Bramley but industrial change was very gradual so their numbers were probably small and the members' concern was restricted to wage improvement.[4] There is no evidence of revolutionary zeal as it was not Bramley Trades Union members, but malcontents marching from Bradford who stopped Bramley's mills in the 1842 Plug Riots.[5] Nor was there any vision or zeal for reform to be found amongst Bramley's richer people, at least as individuals. Abraham Musgrave, a Bramley eccentric, property-owner and money-lender left a fortune of £100,000 when he died in 1862 at the age of 84.[6] During his life his contribution to the improvement of Bramley was to organise a collection for a new organ for the Anglican *Bramley Chapel*.[7] Other rich residents failed to act as individuals, though most would usually contribute to good causes.

With neither secular corporate bodies nor rich individuals ready to initiate improvement any progress derived from the churches and, as Parsons notes, was of a broadly educational nature.

Until 1850 scant provision for the week-day education of the poor existed. During the eighteenth and early nineteenth centuries, at any one time eight poor children could be taught to read, free of charge, alongside middle class children whose parents, presumably, paid a fee, in the *Bramley Chapel School*.[8] In 1825 the appointment of an extra teacher enabled an additional six poor girls to be taught to knit, sew and read.[9] Five years later an unknown writer argued strongly against any further increase in the numbers of poor children in the school.[10] It was argued that those middle class parents who could not afford to educate their children outside Bramley would no longer find places available in the *Chapel School*. Evidently the middle classes mattered more than the poor for there was no increase in the number of places allotted to the poor. Whilst the middle classes were partly catered for and a few poor children were educated free of charge few, if any, children of the working classes would seem to have had any week-day education.

Consequently such children had to rely on Sunday Schools until almost 1850.[11] It is possible that Bramley Anglicans founded a Sunday School in 1789, for in that year particularly large donations, including £20 from the Earl of Cardigan, the absentee landlord of a large part of Bramley, were made to *Bramley Chapel School*.[12] The Baptists began Sunday School classes in 1811 when the then minister, the Reverend Trickett, urged action on behalf of the children of ungodly neighbours and adults who could not read.[13]

Figure 1. Location of Bramley. *Author's collection*

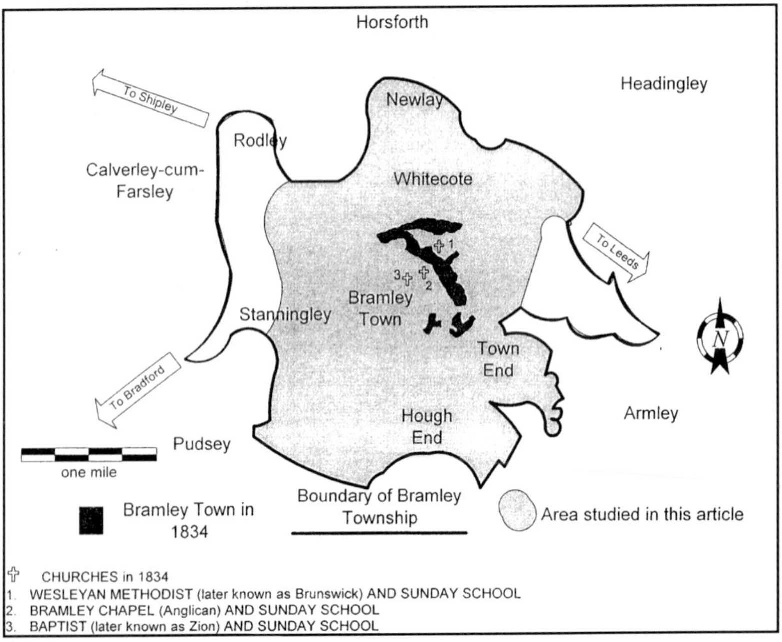

CHURCHES in 1834
1. WESLEYAN METHODIST (later known as Brunswick) AND SUNDAY SCHOOL
2. BRAMLEY CHAPEL (Anglican) AND SUNDAY SCHOOL
3. BAPTIST (later known as Zion) AND SUNDAY SCHOOL

Much later B Grant stated that the Sunday School was designed as a feeder for the chapel.[14] The prime aim then, was to spread the gospel but to meet this aim children had to be able to read *The Bible*, so reading had to be taught. A room next to the chapel had been built to accommodate the Sunday School classes by 1815 and within a few years two stories were added.[15] The Wesleyan Methodists had held Sunday School classes in a rented building from 1806 until a purpose built Sunday School opened in 1821 (Figure 2). Between 1806 and 1821 the classes depended upon funds from an annual collection from Methodists including John Haley and Thomas Pawson (the two builders of New Mills) and from members of other denominations including Charles Lord and John Rogerson (part mill owners).[16] The Baptist congregation comprised predominately artisans and poorer people; their Sunday School was probably built without large individual financial contributions.[17] The Methodists were more fortunate. Amongst their number were rich people including Joshua Burton who made a significant financial contribution to the building of the Sunday School.[18] The Methodists also drew in contributions from Anglicans such as Joseph Rogerson (part mill owner). One surprise was that John Haley made no contribution; indeed he had stopped contributing to the Sunday School classes in 1815, about the time his *Waterloo Mills* was built. The Primitive Methodists opened *Moriah Chapel* in 1835 and either from then or soon after, Sunday School classes were held.[19] A substantial school building was opened in 1865.[20]

It is one thing to provide education: it is quite another to provide effective education. As ever keeping order was no easy task. Wesleyan Sunday School teachers had to track down suspected truants and set work to the unpunctual.[21] Early in 1825 superintendents were concerned that the school was very noisy and this may have led them to establish a set of rules. Naughty pupils, one went so far as to strike a teacher, were excluded for bad conduct but would usually be re-admitted following a promise of future good behaviour. Not everyone would comply. One boy walked out after refusing to do a task for bad conduct. The boy's parents wanted him to be re-admitted but this most obstinate boy refused to apologise, picked up his hat and stalked off. Some of the works Wesleyan pupils were required to read might seem to have contributed to disorder. *Religion and Death* or *The Young Mourner* scarcely seem tempting fare for the young. Yet they had some relevance at a time when death was never far away. And *The Negro's Complaint* or *The Negro's Prayer* might be perceived as introducing pupils to a world outside Bramley.

Anglican and Baptist teachers probably had no easier time than their Wesleyan counterparts. In 1831 the Anglicans spent almost as much on rewards to the children as they did in paying fees to the school master and school mistress.[22] One Baptist teacher kept his classes quiet by reading *Robinson Crusoe* to them.[23] But at least the Baptists encouraged in their scholars a sense of foresight and thrift when, in 1835, they established a *Sunday School Funeral Brief*.[24] This was an insurance paid to parents or friends on the death of a member. Furthermore the efforts made by Sunday School teachers to keep discipline paved the way for the growth of a more orderly society when former scholars became adults.

Scripture, reading and writing were taught in the early Sunday Schools.[25] The Reverend Humphreys, perpetual curate of *Bramley Chapel* from 1821 to 1830, was the son of a labourer and an advocate for the education of the working classes. He encouraged the teaching of reading and writing in *Bramley Chapel Sunday School*.[26] Unfortunately the succeeding incumbent, the Reverend Furbank, was most strongly against the teaching of writing in Sunday Schools and forbade it in *Bramley Chapel School* in 1834.[27] He tried to persuade the non-conformists to follow suit but it is not known if he achieved this aim. Little evidence exists as to how successful was the teaching of Scripture but there is some, albeit small, evidence in respect to reading and writing.

There is, for example, the testimony of a sometime Methodist preacher Joseph Barker, born and bred in Bramley. He insisted his initial learning came from attending Sunday School because, as he records, 'when we had work, we had no time to go to school; and when we had not work, we had nothing with which to pay school wages.'[28]

The Baptists must have achieved some success for otherwise there would have been little point in establishing a Sunday School

Figure 2. Wesleyan Day and Sunday School Building. The lower story dates from 1821, the upper from 1836. *Author's collection*

library.[29] This opened in 1832 and only religious works were to be stocked; but the idea of what was religious was widely interpreted. A subscriber could borrow Milton's *Poetic* works, a Natural History volume, Herchel's *Astronomy* and all four volumes of Lyell's *Principles of Geology*. The library, like the *Sunday School Funeral Brief* continued into the twentieth century.

Given the difficulties with which Sunday School teachers, of any denomination, had to contend, it is scarcely conceivable that, until well after 1850, they would continue to teach unless they were achieving some degree of success. In 1831 just over two hundred children attended the *Bramley Chapel Sunday School*.[30] During the 1820's about 260 children were enrolled and some eighty teachers served in the Wesleyan Sunday School; the addition of an upper story to the school in 1836 substantially increased the numbers who could be taught (Figure 2).[31] The Primitive Methodists had a schoolroom below their chapel and as the Baptists had by 1844, a total of 440 scholars and teachers, it is evident that a very high proportion of Bramley's children attended Sunday School between 1830 and 1850.[32] Sunday Schools offered cheap mass education but their very nature brought disadvantages. With only weekly attendance children could readily forget that which they had learnt in the previous week. Some children would not attend; others could not attend, worn out with long hours of weekday work.[33]

Various Central Government measures, including a sharp reduction in the hours a child under thirteen years could work, were introduced between 1833 and 1846 to encourage day schools to be built. No doubt it was the prospect of grants towards the building of schools and towards teachers' salaries that convinced the Anglicans to build a day school but they showed a strange lack of foresight by building *two* National Schools (namely *Whitecote* and *Bramley*) within a period of only two years.[34] The location of *Whitecote*

National School, on a steep slope and away from the town, was singularly ill-chosen and consequently soon after *Bramley National School*, located near the Town Centre, opened in 1850, *Whitecote* closed (Figure 5).[35] About 1866 the Whitecote building re-opened as a *Middle Class School* but it lost money and so closed about 1876.[36]

Figure 3. Bramley National School. This building is now demolished. The photograph shows the building that opened in 1850. *Author's collection*

Bramley National School (Figure 3) was sited on land donated by the Earl of Cardigan but church members still had to contribute towards building costs; John Lister (owner of *Elmfield Mill*) gave £100.[37] Managers of the school not only had to be in communion with the Church of England but each had to contribute either not less than 20/- a year for at least two years or a dowry of £20. The School was to serve *Children and Adults or Children only of the labouring, manufacturing and other poorer classes of the Chapel of Bramley*. An infants room with a glass roof, was added to the National School building in 1871 and eighteen years later a large building for boys was added.[38] With these improvements up to 812 pupils could be taught.[39] Table one lists the first managers.

Table 1: The first managers of Bramley National School[40]

Name	Occupation
Rev Thomas Furbank	Perpetual Curate
George Nash	Assistant Curate
John Lister	Woollen Mill Owner
Simeon Musgrave	Wool Merchant
John Wilson	Grocer?
Samuel Lister Booth	Solicitor
Robert Clough	Grocer
Richard Nickols	Tanner
Thomas Wade	Stone Merchant

The Anglicans opened a school-church in 1868 to serve Hough End, one of Bramley's settlement outposts (Figure 1).[41] Hough End school was closed when the Anglicans opened *Good Shepherd School* in 1896 at Bramley Town End (Figure 4) with the unfortunate consequence that Hough End children had a much longer walk to school.[42]

A Weslyan School, in some form or other, was in existence by 1847 but the first record of a Wesleyan School offering day time education

Figure 4. The Good Shepherd National School Building. It is no longer a school. *Author's collection*

for the poor occurs in 1850.[43]

Table 2: Managers of the Wesleyan School, 1850 [44]

Name	Occupation
John Lupton	Cloth Manufacturer
James Proctor	Gentleman
Thomas Smithson	Cloth Manufacturer
Richard Wilson	Wine Merchant
Joseph Wood	Gentleman

In that year the managers of the Wesleyan School sought and were awarded a Parliamentary Grant for the Education of the Poor. If the premises were not available from 8.30am to 5.30pm five days a week and if the school were not open for inspection at all reasonable times, the luckless managers had to repay the whole or part of the grant.

Reading, writing and arithmetic were the foundations not only of the 1850 *Bramley National School* curriculum but of elementary education for the next hundred years (Table 3).

Table 3: Subjects Offered and/or Taught in the following schools

in year of	Bramley National 1850	Wesleyan 1879	Hough Lane Board 1888-99	Bramley National 1945-47 (for 7 to 9 year olds)
Scripture	√	√	√	√
Writing. Handwriting	√	√	√	√
Spelling		√	√	√
Composition			√	√
English Grammar	√	√	√	√
Reading	√	√	√	√
Recitation		√	√	
English Literature		√		
Arithmetic	√	√	√	√
Euclid and/or Algebra		√	√	
History	√	√	√	√
Geography	√	√	√	√
Mapping	√		√	
Nature Study/Animal Physiology		√		√
Music/Singing		√	√	√
Art/Drawing	√	√	√	√
Craft/Needlework/				
Domestic Economy		√	√	√
PT			√	√
Bookkeeping		√		
French		√		

(Sources for Table 3 are given in reference) [45]

Art or drawing, history and geography were other mainstays. Late in the nineteenth century geography was a Wesleyan Day School strength as the then headmaster, John Hewit Tomlin, was a geographer.[46] Plans of Bramley and district, wall maps, pictures and a globe were amongst the several fine items of geographical equipment.[47] Tomlin was joint author of several school books. Two of these were used as readers in the school thus anticipating, by a century or more, the claim that geography and history can promote the learning of literacy in primary schools. Perhaps the most striking feature of the subjects shown in Table 3 is the absence of experimental science. Some though, was taught in object lessons at the *Town Street Board School* in the 1890s.[48]

An important caveat must be made as to the curriculum of both the *Bramley National School* in 1850 and the *Wesleyan Day School* in 1879. In both schools different fees were charged and in the *National School* the subjects that could be studied were reflected in the fee structure.[49] This may also have been true of the Wesleyans. Accordingly it seems likely that some, perhaps many, parents would opt to pay only for reading, writing and arithmetic.

Nor was this the only factor hindering the effectiveness of the schools. It was not until 1880 that parents were compelled to have their children educated. So, whilst the *Bramley National School* could, in 1855 accommodate 400 children, only 180 were registered and actual daily attendance fell far lower.[50] Poor attendance by the scholars and a disgraceful lesson by a pupil teacher led to loss of the Government Grant in 1856; indeed it took almost twenty years, after opening, before the Inspectors' reports became favourable.[51] Though in 1873 both *Hough End School* and *Bramley National School* received good reports for their children's learning, pupils' irregular attendance cost *Bramley National School* about £700 over the four years 1871-75.[52] No wonder prizes were awarded for good attendance. And though in 1873, *National School* boys were advised to *persevere in their good conduct and then they would grow up good useful members of society* inevitably lapses happened.[53] In 1881 police action was required to stop snow ball fights between scholars of the various schools.[54]

The immediate cause of the closure of the *Wesleyan Day School* in 1890 was the financial loss it incurred.[55] This had arisen partly through several years of what were then deemed to be excessive staff costs and partly by the award of a much reduced grant in 1890. In turn this resulted from the low standard of pupils' work particularly in the Infants Division.

Despite the difficulties and inadequacies that attended both the

Bramley National and *Wesleyan Day Schools,* for them to have survived the thirty years, from 1850 to 1880, during which education was neither compulsory nor free of charge, does indicate that the Schools had some degree of successful teaching.

Following Forster's *1870 Education Act,* a *Bramley Board* school opened in 1872.[56] It was located in *Moriah Primitive Methodist School* until purpose built premises opened five years later in Hough Lane (Figure 5 and 6).[57] When the *Wesleyan Day School* closed the school rooms were rented to accommodate a new *Town Street Board School* until premises for that school opened in Broad Lane in 1900.[58] Religious premises were not only used to house state schools but the

Figure 5. The Location of Churches and Schools within Bramley Town 1892. *Author's collection*

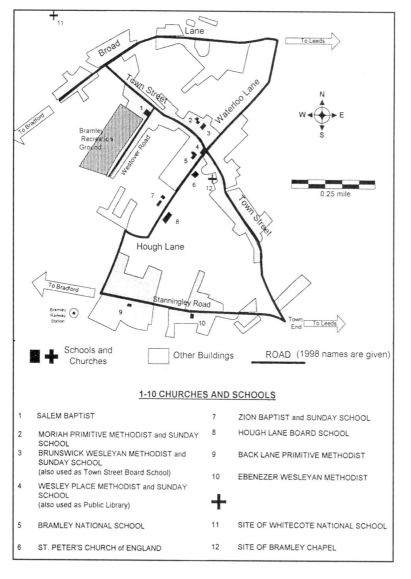

1-10 CHURCHES AND SCHOOLS

1	SALEM BAPTIST	7	ZION BAPTIST and SUNDAY SCHOOL
2	MORIAH PRIMITIVE METHODIST and SUNDAY SCHOOL	8	HOUGH LANE BOARD SCHOOL
3	BRUNSWICK WESLEYAN METHODIST and SUNDAY SCHOOL (also used as Town Street Board School)	9	BACK LANE PRIMITIVE METHODIST
4	WESLEY PLACE METHODIST and SUNDAY SCHOOL (also used as Public Library)	10	EBENEZER WESLEYAN METHODIST
5	BRAMLEY NATIONAL SCHOOL	11	SITE OF WHITECOTE NATIONAL SCHOOL
6	ST. PETER'S CHURCH of ENGLAND	12	SITE OF BRAMLEY CHAPEL

first Bramley public library, opened in 1874, was located in a school room of another *Bramley Methodist Chapel* namely *Wesley Place* (Figure 5).[59]

The Board Schools' curriculum was similar to that of the *Wesleyan School* (Table 3) so rather than offering a different education the Board Schools merely enabled more children to be educated. Though provision increased, the impact of state education in the nineteenth century was limited not only by its late start but by the low proportion (just over a quarter in 1889) of children who attended *Bramley Board School* until 1890.[60] *Bramley National School* claimed to be better than the *Board School* in that its religious instruction was made real; pupils were more select (as fees were higher) and teachers showed a deeper personal interest in children.[61]

Moreover the *Board School* was no more efficient than *Bramley National School* and Board School teachers had their share of difficulties. In the Infants division Miss Boyle, the division's only certificated teacher, had first to insist upon cleanliness and discipline.[62] In the latter respect she was not entirely helped by her three pupil teachers not one of whom could, at one period, keep order.

In both the infants and the mixed school pupil attendance was not good.[63] Sickness and storms took their toll and so too did blatant truancy. The mixed school had its staff problems including an assistant teacher who was too partial to striking pupils on the head and another assistant who was deemed over familiar with a pupil teacher. Pupil attainment varied from class to class and subject to

subject. Some pupils read without any understanding. In 1890 the arithmetic of Standard One was very backward with *no less than 20 failing in a class of 35. Nine of them with every sum wrong.* As long ago as 1888 girls were stated to outshine boys.

By the time the second *Town Street Board School* opened it was a legal requirement for children aged between five and ten to attend school and fees were about to be abolished. Hence attendance, despite some individual truancy, was better than in the early Board

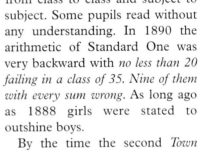

Figure 6. Hough Lane Board School Building now no longer a school.
Author's collection

School years.[64] Order seems to have improved though Bramley pupils still had to be treated with respect! One girl and her sister left the second *Town Street Board School* for the Church School when the girl was told that her hair was as *rough as a terriers* by her teacher.[65] One *Town Street Board School* head, Walter Thurston, seems to have been progressive as he wanted children to make an individual effort in class and he held a series of cricket matches, boys versus girls, which raised interest. He took children on outings to Otley Chevin but *Bramley National School* went one better with outings for older children to either Ingleton or Malham.[66]

Inspectors found the *teaching is thorough and results are very good at Town Street Board School* in 1899.[67] If the inspectors expectations had not altered, *Hough Lane Board School* boys had a higher level of attainment in 1899 than 1888 and with the improvements at *Bramley National School,* Bramley children were at last receiving a sound, if basic, education.[68] But it had taken the best part of a century for this to be achieved.

Meanwhile, in mid-century, the non-denominational *Mechanics Institute* (opened 1845) provided educational opportunities for those whose education had been limited or non-existent when they were younger. In 1863, annual membership fees were four and five shillings.[69] For that money there was access to occasional lectures, newspapers and periodicals and to 989 library books. Pupils were also taught in classes. Certainly the Institute offered good opportunities for further education but relatively few took advantage and, of those who did, the overwhelming majority were male.

Less formal, but no less male dominated, was the short-lived Bramley Discussion Society (1846-52).[70] Primarily recreational it was also incidentally educational. On the lighter side issues debated included: *Whether is a single or married life the most happy.* More serious were: *The English Government ought not to provide for the education of the people* and, *Ought not the suffrage to be extended to every man of sane mind and un-convicted of crime?*

For most adults, free time, if any, was passed when not by the fireside, in either the alehouse or the church (Figures, 7, 8 and 9). If the record in The Roll of the Baptist Church is complete, a change in church attitudes began about 1829.[71] At any time non-attendance was a reason for exclusion from the Baptist church membership but if non-attendance is ignored it would seem that prior to 1829 exclusions were very rare (one is recorded in 1809 for theft) but thereafter exclusions became much more frequent. Baptists no longer solely sought to save souls for the afterlife but also became

Figure 7. Zion Baptist Chapel. This was the new chapel opened in 1846 and existed until the late 1970's when it was substantially altered. *Author's collection*

Figure 8. The *Old Unicorn* public house. Now demolished it was located on Stocks Hill near the present *Old Unicorn* public house. *Author's collection*

concerned with character and conduct in this life. In the early days of the Sunday School scholars had drunk beer; tea was said to be too expensive; likewise at their Easter Feast the Methodist scholars had drunk beer in the early years but in 1824 tea was substituted.[72] From 1829 drunkenness became a common cause for the exclusion of males from the Baptist Chapel.

Interestingly, this began before the temperance movement reached Bramley in 1833.[73] Lawson records that in Pudsey the chapels did not regard the movement with favour.[74] The position in Bramley is unclear but in 1862 the Reverend Colcroft (Baptist Minister) was

Figure 9. *The Cardigan Arms.* This building is now demolished. *Author's collection*

President of the Temperance Society and at some uncertain date the Wesleyans allowed the school to be used by teetotallers.[75] The renowned *Bramley Temperance Brass Band*, which started in 1837, consisted of working men so the temperance movement was an added force for improvement.[76]

To return to The Roll, sinful conduct led to both females and males being excluded from the chapel and even associating with loose young men led, along with drunkenness, to one male member being excluded. Falsehood and disorderly conduct were other reasons for exclusion. It might be argued that as there were so many exclusions the chapel was failing. If it was failing some members, it was also encouraging others to enjoy a more orderly and moral life. Late in the century the Wesleyans were also helping to inculcate orderliness.[77] Breaches of their choir rules led choristers to be disciplined: in 1890 six choristers were admonished for forming a glee club. Foundations for better adults were laid in the young. All denominations, for example, had a *Band of Hope* aiming at encouraging sobriety and truth.

As the century advanced church roles widened further. Most of the members of a Lacrosse Club were young Wesleyans so, in 1883, the club was permitted to meet on church premises.[78] The Reverend Gott (Anglican) was largely responsible for convincing the City Council to buy land to create a recreation ground (only the second in Leeds), and it was he who started a *Mothers' Meeting and Church Institute*.[79] Institute members had opportunities to read newspapers and magazines, to select from a library of 500 volumes, to play games including bagatelle and chess, to partake in an annual day trip - the

Figure 10. Some members of the respectable working classes, about 1914. The man on the extreme right is a local official of some lodge.
Author's collection

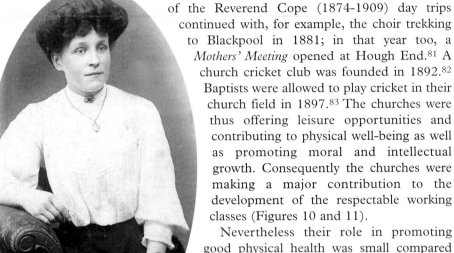

venue in 1873 was Scarborough.[80] During the curacy of the Reverend Cope (1874-1909) day trips continued with, for example, the choir trekking to Blackpool in 1881; in that year too, a *Mothers' Meeting* opened at Hough End.[81] A church cricket club was founded in 1892.[82] Baptists were allowed to play cricket in their church field in 1897.[83] The churches were thus offering leisure opportunities and contributing to physical well-being as well as promoting moral and intellectual growth. Consequently the churches were making a major contribution to the development of the respectable working classes (Figures 10 and 11).

Nevertheless their role in promoting good physical health was small compared with secular bodies. In this sphere Leeds Corporation played the greatest role when it brought mains water supply to Bramley in 1860 and mains sewage disposal in the 1870s.[84] Deaths from cholera occurred in 1849 (Figure 12) and in the 1860s Bramley had a high death rate, attributed to inadequate sanitation, so the Corporation had certainly taken its time.[85] But connecting piped water and sewers to individual properties was a gradual process; as late as 1894 closets were still being linked to mains sewerage.[86] In promoting improved health the role of the Co-operative Society must not be neglected.

Figure 11. Louisa Tiffany (nee Dixon) was the daughter of a Blacksmith. She attended Hough End School where she was awarded a prize for general knowledge.
Author's collection

Figure 12. The inscription of a gravestone, located in Bramley Baptist Burial Ground, states:
Sacred to the memory of Malley Daughter of John and Mary Pawson who died of Cholera Sept. 1st 1849 8 years.
Author's collection

When a *Leeds Co-operative Society* was proposed early in 1847 George Dawson become one of the very few Bramley men to risk a guinea to join. Dawson was so keen a member of the Co-operative movement that he was prepared to walk from Bramley to Leeds and back after a full day's work in order to attend meetings of the *Society*.[87] Perhaps it was through Dawson's influence that Bramley was the chosen location for the very first Leeds co-operative flour shop, in 1847 (Figure 13). At a stroke workers could obtain unadulterated flour and flour at a low price. Other Bramley grocers had to lower their prices to compete, so everyone except the grocers gained. As health improved death rates fell so contributing to Bramley's population growth.

Secular bodies also played a part in creating a more orderly society. Towards the end of 1831 an association for the *Detection and Prosecution of Felons and Misdemeanours in Bramley* was formed but it seems to have lain dormant until 1841 when a formal document was signed and sealed for this purpose by almost all the tradesmen and mill-owners of Bramley[88]. Notices were posted offering rewards for the detection of crime, for example £10 reward was offered for establishing the names of those who slaughtered and carried away a fine fat sheep belonging to butcher Hargreaves. The society ceased in 1860 following a contretemps amongst some members but in any event had become largely superfluous for in 1857 paid full-time constabulary were established in Bramley and for the rest of the century were to play an important part in maintaining order.[89]

Notwithstanding the importance of a paid constabulary, the churches initially through their schools and then through their expectations of adult behaviour were equally, if not more, significant in creating respectable members of the working classes. And it was the churches who played the key role in the spread of literacy in Bramley. In so doing, individuals were enabled to further their education at a period when print was so dominant as a source of concepts and information. Accordingly the churches emerge as beacons of working class advancement.

Figure 13. First flour agents shop, Stocks Hill, Bramley which opened 1847.

Notes and References

1. Parsons, E *The Civil, Ecclesiastical, Literary, Commercial and Miscellaneous History of Leeds*, Vol. I, 1834, p 195.

2. Carr, ET (ed.) *The Lands of Bram.*, 1937, p 11.

3. Hennock, EP *Fit and Proper Persons*, 1973, pp 190-192 and pp 196-197.

4. *The Leeds Mercury*, 15.12.1832.

5. Mayhall, J *The Annals of Yorkshire*, Vol. I, p 483.

6. Mayhall, J *The Annals of Yorkshire*, Vol. II, p 54.

Yorkshire Post, 1.5.1906.

7. Rogerson, J *Diaries for 1808-09 and 1811-14*, Entry for 7.11.1812. Printed in Crump W.B. (ed.) *The Leeds Woollen Industry 1780-1820* XXX11, 1931, p 145 Thoresby Society - hereafter Thors. Soc. Note: Between 1800 and 1861 the Anglican place of worship was called the Chapel of St. Margaret of Antioch. In this article it is called Bramley Chapel, the name frequently used at that period. In 1863 a new building for Anglican worship opened and was called The Church of St. Peter. It is still in use in 1998.

8. Unnamed and undated (but probably soon after 1830) account of Bramley Chapel School. Bundle 173, West Yorkshire Archive Service, hereafter, WYAS, Leeds. Unnamed letter, dated 1.6.1830. Bundle 173, WYAS Leeds.

9. Humphreys, R and Tattersall, P A letter of 18.2.1825 sent to Waite, W and Musgrave, S Bundle 173, WYAS Leeds. Unnamed and undated account, *op.cit.*

10. Unnamed letter dated 1.6.1830, *op.cit.*

11. From 1800 to 1835 there were only the Anglican, Baptist and Wesleyan Methodist Chapels (Figure 1). In 1836 a Primitive Methodist Chapel opened. Between 1852 and 1892 other churches opened (Figure 5). However as day schools developed from 1848 the role of Sunday Schools as providers of non-religious education declined. So this article concentrates upon the Anglican, Baptist and Wesleyan Methodist Chapels; little has been traced about the early Primitive Methodist Sunday Schools.

12. Subscribers for Bramley Chapel School, 1789. Bundle 173, WYAS, Leeds.

13. *Pudsey and Stanningley News*, 13.10.1911.

14. Grant, B As reported in the *Pudsey Advertiser*, 12.10.1911.

15. *Pudsey and Stanningley News*, 13.10.1911.

16. Committee for the Intended Sunday School by Gratuous Teachers, 1806. Box 31D4 Thors. Soc.

Sunday School Accounts, 1821-4. Box 31D4 Thors. Soc.

Silson, A Bramley Takes Off in *Aspects of Leeds 1 Discovering Local History*, edited by Stevenson Tate, L 1998 pp 125-142.

17. The Roll, Baptist Church, Bramley. Privately Held.

Wardle and Bentham, *Commercial Directory*, 1814-15.

Pigot, Commercial Directory, 1818-20.

Gravestones, of people who had been alive 1815, located in the Baptist Burial Ground.

18. Sunday School Accounts, *op.cit.*

A Survey and Valuation of all the Mills, Land and Quarries in the Township of Bramley. Hepworth and Son, 1823, pp 35-44. WYAS, Lo B5, Leeds.

19. Moriah Primitive Methodist Chapel Bramley *Souvenir of Centenary Bazaar*, 23.2.1910 to 26.2.1910

20. *ibid.*

Bramley Almanac, 1880.

Beckworth, W A *Book of Remembrance. Records of Leeds Primitive Methodism*, 1910 p 150 gives the date as 1866.

21. This paragraph is based upon evidence to be found in *The Superintendant's (sic) Memorandum Book*, 1824-1830 Reference 386, WYAS, Leeds. This book does not name the Sunday School but there is sufficient evidence, including the names of the Superintendents, to identify it as the Wesleyan Sunday School.

22. Bramley National Sunday School Report, 1831. Bundle 173, WYAS, Leeds.

23. A speech given by Northrop, M and reported in the *Pudsey and Stanningley News*, 13.10.1911.

24. Rules of the Bramley Zion Baptist Sunday School Brief. Privately held.

25. Committee for the Intended Sunday School by Gratuous Teachers *op.cit.*

Pudsey Advertiser, 12.10.1911. This report also states arithmetic was taught at the Baptist Sunday School but no supporting evidence has been traced.

Grant, B A *History of Zion Baptist Sunday School*, 1889.

Unnamed author. *A History of Bramley Church*, 1878 p 22.

26. Unnamed author. *A History of Bramley Church*, *op.cit* p22.
Dobson, A *A History Of The Ancient Chapel of Bramley from 1200 and Of The Church Of St. Peter 1863-1963*, 1964 p 29.
27. Furbank, T *On the Impropriety of Teaching Writing in Sunday Schools on The Lord's Day*, 1832. Bundle 173, WYAS, Leeds.
A History of Bramley Church, 1878, *op.cit.* p 22.
28. Barker, J *The Life Of Joseph Barker*, MDCCCLXXX pp 34-35.
29. This paragraph is based on *The Minute Book of Bramley Baptist Sunday School Library*, 1831. Privately held.
30. Bramley National Sunday School Report, *op.cit.*
31. The Superintendant's Memorandum Book, *op.cit.*
Hill, J *Memorials of Methodism*, 1859, p 21.
32. Beckworth, W *op.cit.* p 150.
Grant, B 1889, *op.cit.*
33. British Parliamentary Papers. *Industrial Revolution. Children's Employment*, Vol. 2, session 1831-1832. *Evidence of Colton, R* pp 124-127.
34. Conveyance of Whitecote National School site on Green Slade to the Archdeacon of Craven and others, 10.3.1847. Reference 229, WYAS, Leeds.
Conveyance of the Earl of Cardigan to the minister and chapelwardens of Bramley, 20.4.1849. Reference 231, WYAS, Leeds.
35. Handbill on the opening of Bramley National Schools, 1850. The University of Leeds Education Museum.
Letter from the Rev S Cope to the National Society. Undated but the evidence suggests 1876. Reference 229, WYAS, Leeds.
36. Letter from the Rev S Cope *op cit.*
37. Conveyance of the Earl of Cardigan, 1849, *op.cit.*
Dobson, A *op.cit* p78.
38. Dobson, A *op.cit.* p 82.
39. Parliamentary Return on Elementary Education for the year ended 31.8.1893. Published, 1894.
40. Conveyance of the Earl of Cardigan, 1849, op.cit.
Census Returns for 1851.
41. Bramley Almanac, 1880.
42. Leeds School Board Log Book of the Bramley Town Street Mixed Department and Broad Lane Council School Mixed Department, 1892-1917. Entry for 27.4.1896. Reference 5/1 WYAS, Leeds.
43. White W. *Directory of Leeds*, 1847
Slater National Directory, 1848
Grants under Minute of 1846. Memorandum of An Agreement 1.4.1850. Bundle Ho 23/11, WYAS, Leeds.
44. Grants under Minute of 1846. Memorandum of An Agreement 1.4.1850. Bundle Ho 23/11, WYAS, Leeds
45. Handbill on the opening of Bramley National Schools, *op.cit.*
Bramley Almanac, 1879.
Log Book of the Leeds Bramley Mixed Board School, 1888. Reference 6/1, WYAS, Leeds.
Bramley St. Peter's School Reports for the school years ending 1946 and 1947. Privately held.
46. *Bramley Almanac*, 1879.
47. Inventory of the Wesleyan Day School, 9.9.1890. Bundle Ho 23/11, WYAS, Leeds.
48. Log Book of Bramley Town Street Mixed Department, *op.cit.* See, for example, the entry of 23.5.1898.
49. Handbill on the opening of Bramley National School, *op.cit.*
Bramley Almanac, 1879.
50. Handbill on the opening of Bramley National Schools, *op.cit.*
Dobson, A *op.cit.* p 80
51. Dobson, A *op cit.*, p 80
52. *Bramley Parish Magazine* for 1873, 1874 and 1875.
53. *Bramley Parish Magazine*, 1873, *op cit*
54. Dobson, A *op.cit.* p 82.
55. This paragraph is based on Mawbey, H *Report on Wesleyan Day School*, Bramley, 1890. Bundle Ho 23/11, WYAS, Leeds.
56. *Bramley Almanac*, 1879.
57. *Bramley County Secondary School Magazine*, July 1967, p 6 and p 7.
58. Memorandum of Agreement for tenancy of Bramley Wesleyan School by Leeds School Board,

22.10.1890. Bundle Ho 23/11, WYAS, Leeds.

Bramley Wesleyan Chapel Secretary's Minute Book, 1868-1921. Entries for 19.7.1890; 24.10.1890; 26.11.1890; 13.9.1900. Reference 23/5, WYAS, Leeds.

59. *Bramley Almanac*, 1880.

Carr, ET *op.cit.*, p 36.

60. Carr, ET *op.cit.*, p 26.

61. *Bramley Parish Magazine*, 1878.

62. Leeds School Board Log Book of Bramley Infants Board School, 1872. Reference 1/1, WYAS, Leeds.

63. Leeds School Board Log Book of Bramley Infants Board School, 1872 *op.cit.*

Log Book of Leeds Bramley Mixed Board School, *op.cit.*

64. Log Book of Leeds Bramley Mixed Board School, *op.cit.*

Log Book of Bramley Town Street Mixed Department, *op.cit.*

65. Log Book of Bramley Town Street Mixed Department, *op.cit.*

66. Log Book of Bramley Town Street Mixed Department, *op.cit.*.

Dobson, A *op.cit.*, p 48.

67. Log Book of Bramley Town Street Mixed Department, *op.cit.*

68. Log Book of Leeds Bramley Mixed Board School, *op.cit.*

69. This paragraph is based on Hole, J *The Working Classes of Leeds*, 1863 especially p 140.

70. This paragraph is based on Minute Book of Bramley Discussion Society. Reference 273, WYAS, Leeds.

71. The Roll *op.cit.*

72. Grant, B 1889 *op.cit.*

Pudsey and Stanningley News, 13.10.1911 *op.cit.*

Committee for the Intended Sunday School by Gratuous Teachers *op.cit.*

Sunday School Accounts, 1821-24 *op.cit.*

73. Bramley Almanac, 1857.

74. Lawson, J *Letters to the Young on Progress in Pudsey*, 1887 r. 1978 p91.

75. Bramley Almanac, 1862.

Brown, S *Bramley Methodist Chapel in 200 Years Of Methodism On The Site of Bramley Trinity*, 1977 p 5.

76. Bramley Almanac, 1860.

77. Bramley Wesleyan Chapel Secretary's Minute Book, op.cit., entry for 21.6.1890.

78. Bramley Wesleyan Chapel Secretary's Minute Book, op.cit., entry for 31.8.1883.

79. Dobson, A op.cit., pp 43-44.

80. *Bramley Parish Magazine*, 1873, *op cit*

81. *Bramley Parish Magazine*, 1881.

82. Dobson, A *op.cit.*, p 50.

83. Minute Book of the Finance Committee of Zion Baptist Chapel, entry for 11.2.1897. Privately held.

84. *Bramley Almanac*, 1870.

Assessment for the Relief of the Poor of the Township of Bramley, 3.11.1864. Reference PL/B3, WYAS, Leeds.

Bramley Almanac, 1863.

Assessment for the Relief of the Poor of the Township of Bramley, 1.9.1870. Reference PL/B3, WYAS, Leeds.

Assessment for the Relief of the Poor of the Township of Bramley in the Bramley Union, 25.11.1880. Reference PL/B3, WYAS, Leeds.

85. Gravestones in the Bramley Baptist Burial Ground.

Bramley Almanac, 1863.

86. Bramley Wesleyan Chapel Secretary's Minute Book, op.cit., entry for 2.3.1894.

87. Holyoake, G *The Jubilee History of the Leeds Industrial Co-operative Society,* 1897 p 176 and pp 250-252.

88. Rules and Regulations for the Prosecution of Persons on Charges of Felony and Misdemeanours. Reference 271, WYAS, Leeds.

89. *Bramley Almanac*, 1863.

10. A YEAR AT ST ANNE'S SCHOOL, WOODHOUSE SQUARE 1952-1953

by Maureen Thorp

I WAS BORN AT HYDE TERRACE maternity hospital, Woodhouse, Leeds. My parents Jack and Anne Flanagan were both born in Leeds. They had four children, Patrick, myself Maureen Frances, my twin brother Michael, and Brian. My twin and I were baptised at the Holy Rosary church, Chapeltown, which was a leafy suburb of Leeds at that time. The Church was adjacent to a splendidly domed Synagogue. Both are still standing, but the Synagogue building is now home to the renowned Northern School of Contemporary Dance.

My father was baptised a Catholic but at the age of three, having lost his mother in the great 'flu epidemic of 1918, he was sent to a local non-Catholic school in Woodhouse. My Grandfather, John Flanagan, who was forty years old at the time of my father's birth, was left with two young children to rear on his own; therefore the children's religious education was more lax than it would have been normally. My Aunt Frances Emmelena (Auntie Lena to we children), who was two years older than my father, later became a practising Anglican. However, my parents did marry according to Catholic rite in St Anne's Cathedral on 30 July 1938.[1] My mother was not a Catholic, but at that time in a 'mixed' marriage, where one parent was a non-Catholic, the couple had to promise that any children of the marriage would be reared in the Catholic faith (Figure 1).

My mother was the youngest of seven children, six girls and a boy, who was the nearest to her in age. She too was raised in a one parent family, as her father had died of pneumonia when she was still in her mother's womb. Her father had been a regular soldier billeted in the local Barracks in Sheepscar. On leaving

Figure 1. Jack and Anne Flanagan on their wedding day 30 July 1938. *Author's collection*

school she went into tailoring. Between the two World Wars, working class girls, if employed at all, almost invariably worked in factories, mills or domestic service.

Mothers were the prime movers in deciding which school or church their children attended, so despite having been baptised into the Catholic faith, we were sent to the local council school, Potternewton Infants and Juniors, which catered for children up to the age of eleven years. This was a must as my mother had four children in two and a half years, and therefore the school had to be near the local amenities. Also, these years were during the Second World War, when my father was away serving as a sergeant in the Royal Enginners, so expediency was the order of the day. My mother died when I and my twin were seven years old, and Brian and Patrick were six and eight respectively. We moved down into the valley of Meanwood, onto what was known as the White House Estate.

This title would perhaps conjure up visions of an estate built in the former grounds of a splendid mansion, known as the White House. The truth however is somewhat more mundane. The houses got their name from the fact that they were more or less white in colour, being of pebble dashed and cement rendered. They were constructed in the 1920s, and were in fact some of Lloyd George's 'homes fit for heroes', being originally intended for the returning soldiers of the First World War. Either because the quality of construction did not match the high ideals of their conception, or for other reasons, the entire estate has now been demolished and replaced by a new estate of brick built houses.

Living on this large estate were two Catholic families who we became quite friendly with. One of them was a family of ten, who introduced my brothers and I to the nearby St Urban's Catholic Church, which was on the border of Headingley and Meanwood. Some of the children went to St Anne's, in Woodhouse Square, near the centre of Leeds, and so it was decided by my father that this then would be an appropriate time to keep the promise made at his marriage ceremony, by sending his three younger children to St Anne's school. My eldest brother Patrick, having reached the age of eleven the previous year, had already moved to Bentley Lane Council School, in Meanwood, and it was decided not to subject him to any further unnecessary change (Figure 2).

The culture shock was enormous on my introduction to a Roman Catholic school. Firstly, there was the matter of being bussed into the heart of Leeds, after being used to walking to the local school at Potternewton across large playing fields with disused quarries.

Secondly, there were the nuns who, unlike the kindly spirits in St Joseph's Home, where my Grandfather had died when I was eight years old, were rather strict and authoritarian. The boys and girls were housed in separate buildings and so, although two of my brothers were also at the school, we were separated for the first time in our young lives.

The Head Teacher of St Anne's School, who was appointed on 7 September 1949, was Sister Margaret (Etheldreda M Wells before taking her vows). Her previous school experience was of managing a school. She had not been there in a teaching capacity. At St Anne's she was to teach as well.[2] This may explain what I perceived to be her rather short temper. I well remember the day that she caned me for going into the park opposite the school. We had been banned from going into this park at lunchtime. Previously we had been allowed to go in, and we would sit on the benches talking to friends who lived in the same neighbourhood, but whom we did not see during classes.

When I started at this school my first term was spent in a small annex unit. This was a prefab just of Clarendon Road (the site is now a car park for the new Dental Institute; situated a few yards away on the opposite side of the road is Claremont House, headquarters of the Yorkshire Archeological Society). Miss Bolton was our teacher.

Figure 2. Brian Patrick, Michael and Maureen Flanagan. *Author's collection*

She was, I think, an exceptional woman, kindly and talented in her role. Miss Kathleen Bolton was appointed as a U-grade teacher on 1 February 1924. She was born 8 December 1898. Miss Bolton retired on 22 July 1955, after thirty-four years at the school.[3] The classification U-grade would seems to be that of unqualified teacher, since to meet post-war needs, a scheme for the emergency training of teachers was introduced after the First World War, and over a period of six years some 35,000 prospective teachers attended one-year courses, some of them in colleges opened specially for the purpose.[4]

Other teachers at that time included Sister Dolores, Miss Carry, Miss Garritt, Miss Sowerby and Miss Sedgewick. The Housecraft tutor was Nurse Brazier, and for Cookery we had Miss Turney. The Managers of St Anne's School were Canon Michael Thorp, the Cathedral's administrator, with Sister Superior.[5] If there are any omissions from this list I must apologise. They are due to my own inadequate memory, and the fact that the records kept at the Diocesan Archives for this particular school year are rather sketchy

I can remember being in a rather confused state in my first term, probably due to the vast changes in my school environment, particularly the loss of contact with my siblings. But I had great fun playing in the small grounds of this prefab and well remember the surnames of the children I played with then, Anderson, Rutherford, McDonald, which gives some insight into their origins.

It was at this school that I developed a social consciousness, and perhaps the seeds were sown of what was to be a growing interest in people and society. There were three incidents that have had a major formative effect on my life. The first concerned a fight between two pupils. I ran with the excitement of the crowd, not out of any interest in the fight, and Miss Bolton saw me there. In the aftermath of the

Figure 3. St Anne's School. *Author's collection*

incident she gave me a real dressing down and I felt so thoroughly ashamed of myself, that I have never run with the crowd since. The second incident is to do with our religious instruction class; we were told that to kill oneself was a mortal sin, and anyone who did do this terrible act would go straight to Hell. I remember thinking that this could not be true, as God would not punish what I perceived to be one of life's victims. The last incident was the hanging of the nineteen year old Derek Bentley on 28 January 1953.[6] This was the first judicial execution of which I was aware, under circumstances which even then gravely perturbed me.

Derek Bentley and Christopher Craig were caught trying to rob a warehouse on 2 November 1952. The evidence was that Craig had shot in the head one of the policemen who had been called when they were spotted on the roof of the warehouse. As Craig was under age at sixteen years, Bentley alone, who was nineteen, was sentenced to hang for the shooting. A plea for clemency for Bentley, an epileptic with learning difficulties, was rejected and he was hanged on 28 January 1953. Craig served fifteen years and was released in 1968.[7] Bentley was posthumously pardoned in 1998. I remember the gloom of the morning of the hanging, the rain shining on the cobble-stones; it seemed that teachers and pupils alike understood the pathos of the day. Subsequently I have developed a strong conviction that killing anyone is morally wrong, be it by an individual or by the State.

After the Autumn term of 1952, I was introduced to the main school, which was not as pleasant to me as there was less freedom, but I found the lessons much easier and acquired the learning bug (Figure 3). The particular classroom I was in housed a set of encyclopaedias which I made full use of, and I could recite the entire British Kings and Queens from their origins to the present day. Perhaps my interest was because the present Queen was due to be crowned, and the festivities were on every one's mind. To me it was like a fairy-tale, the Princess Elizabeth was exquisite, and the whole spectacle of the coronation was mingled with the images of those 'Queens' of the big screen, such a Virginia Mayo and Maureen O'Hara, and the Walt Disney films of *Snow White* and *Cinderella*.

The main school itself was situated in Woodhouse Square. It had outside toilets and no facilities for school meals. We therefore at mid-day went to St Andrew's School, which was situated at the side of Park Lane, on a steep hill. It has now been sympathetically redeveloped into office premises. We would walk crocodile fashion around the corner from the Square, past the old Park Lane Board School (now the site of Park Lane FE College, which was opened by

Margaret Thatcher), and cross Park Lane near to the shops and the old Rutland pub, now renamed the *Fox and Newt*. On we went to reach St Andrew's at the corner of Park Lane and St Andrew's street. We chatted amongst ourselves and had a very pleasant time during the walk. We followed the same route back to school. At other times we would use what I remember as St George's School, which was in the opposite direction, passing the park and following the road going down the hill next to Marlbeck tailoring factory, opposite St George's Church and Crypt. This was in the years before the inner city ring road network was built (Figure 4-6).

We also had music lessons in the annexe in front of the main entrance to St George's church. St George's church and the annexe still stand today but the old school of St George's has long since gone. The music lessons mainly consisted of singing. We learned the school song there. It was in praise of St Anne the Mother of Mary, the bearer of Jesus Christ, and the school that bears her name. I still remember the words verbatim:

> *Come let us sing the song of our school*
> *We'll sing it's praises with joy and zest*
> *We'll raise up a song to great St Anne*
> *Our school bears her name, she is our patroness.*
>
> *For each of us is her salvation, we are proud to bear her name.*
> *No empty title is given our school, it's glorious name we proclaim,*

Figure 4. Map showing the main sites used by St Anne's School. *Redrawn by David Wycherley from Ordnance Survey 1:25000 1908*

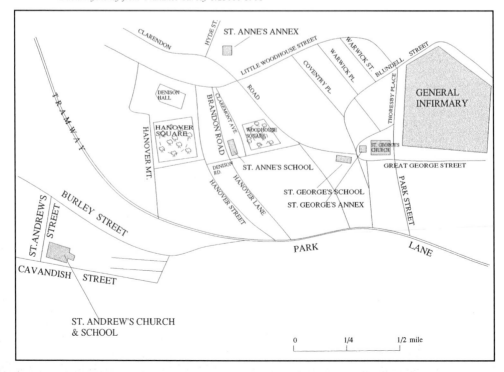

Figure 5. St Andrew's School, Burley Road. *Author's collection*

So sing, sing, call upon her the mother of her who's son is the King.

We also went to hear Chamber Music concerts, which gave me a taste for heavier music. Not being *au-fait* with the inner city of Leeds, having spent my early years in the Potternewton area, I now have no idea where these events occurred, but it was possibly Salem Church. Nor can I remember where all the pupils at St Anne's had to go to be immunised against tuberculosis. All I remember was being in a very long queue (probably in Park Square), and examining our arms where we had had the injection when we got back to school and in the days that followed. I took like a duck to water when it came to learning about Catholicism. It consumed me because religion is essentially about people and ideas and their relationship with God. This developed in me a social conscience and the ability

Figure 6. St George's Annex. *Author's collection*

Figure 7. Bishop Heenan.
Courtesy of Leeds Diocesan Office

to think about issues. It also led me to taking my first Holy Communion, and I remember with pleasure going to Schofield's. a high class store in Leeds, to purchase the lovely white dress which I wore for that one occasion. Schofield's was one of those family owned institutions which alas have today disappeared from Leeds, the name commemorated by a modern shopping precinct on the site. And I remember later my Confirmation also at St Urban's Church, Brookfield Road. The parish Priest was Father Eugene Teahan and I was confirmed by the then Bishop Heenan of Leeds. He was later to become Archbishop and eventually Cardinal Heenan. I thought him to be a man of great compassion, a man who loved his fellow men (Figure 7).

At my Confirmation Bishop Heenan asked the children who were to be confirmed *'Why do we use the Latin language in our services?'* Nobody had an answer, so the Bishop answered *'It is because Latin is a dead language. It therefore never changes'* and this appealed to me. I particularly loved going to Benediction on a Sunday evening; it had a particular magic for me because the service was in Latin. It was mysterious to me as I wasn't tutored in Latin, but it was enough to know that we were praising God. I still have my certificate of Confirmation and feel proud to have been confirmed by such a special person as Bishop Heenan.

The school paid regular visits to St Anne's Cathedral, which I loved and still visit regularly, it being a special place for me. As a child of eleven or twelve years old, I had never seen anything so beautiful. The whole ambience of the place still thrills me. But I miss the Latin Mass and feel that the ceremony of the Mass has been diminished by the changes after the Second Vatican Council in 1962-65.

Another more mundane pleasure, whilst at St Anne's was the purchase of pikelets (crumpets) at the large window of one of an adjacent row of terraced houses. Steaming hot and costing an old halfpenny, they were cheap and nourishing for a growing child. The people who owned the business went on to become well known and respected members of the community, due to their notable time as councillors. Their names were May and Albert Sexton.

All this was at a time when Britain was rapidly recovering from the gloom of the war years. The early death of the well-loved King had been a tragedy for the nation, but we were to have a radiant new Queen. During the preparations for the forthcoming Coronation, there came the death of the late King's mother Queen Mary, at the age of eighty-five, on Tuesday 24 March 1953. She lay in state in Westminster Hall, and some 70,000 people filed past to pay their last respects.[9] The *Yorkshire Evening News* that week mentioned Queen Mary's visit to Leeds, when she opened the Civic Hall in 1938. In the same newspaper on 8 May, Clifford Lackey gave details of readers hints on 'How to decorate your street'.[10]

The Leeds Civic officials celebrated the Coronation with a programme of events which started on Friday 1 May and continued until Monday 31 August. The Lord Mayor and Lady Mayoress were Alderman Frank B Burnley and Mrs H E Weaver, who were in office from May 1952 to May 1953. Alderman Donald G Cowling MBE JP and Mrs Cowling became Lord Mayor and Lady Mayoress on 18 May 1953.[11] One of these events was the annual Children's Day which in 1953 was held on 4 July[12]. It was always held on a Saturday and was an event full of pageantry and skill. The children of many Leeds schools participated in this event; some schools would produce a tableau or animated display, known as a 'float' mounted on the back of a lorry. Events commenced with a grand parade of the floats; the lorries, accompanied by various 'official' vehicles, drove slowly up the Headrow through the centre of Leeds, and then out through the suburbs to Roundhay Park. The route of the parade was lined with spectators, the Headrow in particular was a mass of people. The activities at the Park centred on the Arena, where the best from the schools competed with one another in athletics; there was colourful dancing of Scottish reels and the highlight was the crowning of the Children's Day Queen by the Lady Mayoress. Because it was Coronation year the 'Queen' of the Children's Day that year, Jacqueline Kneeshaw, had eight attendants and a new crown to mark the event; the crown was paid for by her attendants (Figure 8-9).[13]

The St Anne's float depicted the three heroes John Hunt, Sherpa Tensing and Edmund Hilary, who were the first conquerors of Everest, on 29 May 1953. The children on the float chanted the following:

When June the second dawned
And Elizabeth was crowned.
Over Everest's mighty peak
The British flag was found.

The three girls chosen to represent the three male heroes of Everest were very convincing - a round faced, dark haired girl for Sherpa Tensing, a taller, fairer girl for John Hunt and an even taller girl to

Figure 8 and 9. Children's Day Parade in Leeds c1960. *Courtesy of E Bews*

represent Edmund Hillary.

On 22 May 1953 the school closed for the Whitsuntide holidays, and re-opened on the 5 June 1953[14]. The holiday was extended from 1 June in honour of the Coronation. On 5 June the pupils and staff of the school celebrated the Coronation by going to Scarborough for the day. We went by a special train at 10.00am and returned at 8.30pm.[15] I still remember the pleasure of the day. It was lovely and sunny and the atmosphere was full of anticipation; for many of the pupils it would be their first sight of the sea. I even remember the sandwiches I took, cheese and tomato, and having a discussion with another pupil about the merits of keeping the tomato intact instead of sliced in the sandwich with the cheese. Further to this special treat all the children in Leeds were presented with a glass mug decorated with the Royal Coat of Arms, and a tin of sweets bearing a portrait of the new Queen.[16]

Mary Mitchell and Kathleen Thompson, two of the girls I became quite friendly with, were both mentioned in St Anne's Log Book: it states that the two girls, both Christmas leavers, were to attend a fortnight's intensive Housecraft Course at Blenheim School. In the period I was at St Anne's I attended cookery lessons at Belle View School (now demolished). Also in the Log Book it states that on 11 March 1953 'A party of Senior girls visited John Barran Ltd Clothing Manufacturer, accompanied by the Headteacher.'[17] When I joined the main school I was seated next to Kathleen Thompson, and she taught me how to count in French; this encouraged me to teach myself some basic words from one of the books on the classroom shelf, as we did not have French lessons.

Two of the 'old boys' of St Anne's were Jimmy Savile and Peter O'Toole. In the *Yorkshire Post* dated Friday 9 November 1984 Jimmy Savile talked about his time spent at the school from the age of four to fourteen. He seems to have enjoyed a very happy time at the school and mentions Peter O'Toole's short period there.[18]

According to the Log Book the supply teacher Miss S Byren ceased duties with no further supply teachers sent, although Miss Bolton was still absent; Sister Margaret amalgamated her own class with Miss Bolton's, making a total of fifty-two girls.[19] Having mentioned previously that Sister Margaret had been an administrator until she came to St Anne's, this may have proved too much for her. She resigned as Headteacher on 31 August 1954, only a year after I had left the school.[20] The then Deputy Headteacher, Sister Dolores (Miss Marie Clapham) had been previously appointed Headteacher on 1 September 1936. The records do not say when or why she relinquished this position. She was re-appointed as Headteacher and took up her duties on 6 September 1954. She served in this position until her retirement on 31 August 1968. Her successor was Sister Anne (Miss M F Smith).[21]

St Anne's is now amalgamated with other Catholic schools in Leeds. What was the main school building is now an annexe of Park Lane College.[22]

Appendices

Although not related to my own time at St Anne's, perhaps readers will be as interested as I was to read two reports of His Majesty's Inspectors of Schools. The first is dated 20 June 1923 typed in the fashion of the time, it reads as follows:

> *INFANTS: This is a bright and well-managed little school. The Headteacher works hard and thoughtfully: she and her staff are properly sympathetic with child life, and the children are happily and actively responsive. Much apparatus for individual work has been made, which gives the children added interest in their lessons.*
>
> *The teaching of English is careful and stimulating: the written compositions at the top of the school are creditable, and good speech training is evident. Correspondingly good progress is made in other subjects.*

Such a report would surely be the envy of many a school today!

The second report is of the school year preceeding my attendance and is dated 1 May 1952 and is again reproduced in the style of the period.

> *GIRL'S DEPARTMENT: This Girls' School adjoins the Infant School on the ground floor of a two-storey building in the centre of Leeds: the Boys' School occupies the upper floor. The site of the building is very restricted: the girls and infants share a small playground the surface of which is in very poor condition. The work of the School is interrupted by noise from the works nearby.*
>
> *At the time of this Inspection there were 152 girls in the School with an age range of six plus to fifteen and organised as far as possible on an age basis into two junior classes, a transition class and two senior classes. Four of these classes are housed in the main building and the fifth, the transition class, uses a H.O.R.S.A hut on a site near the School where a small garden has also been developed. All the rooms in the main building are separated by movable wood and glass partitions and it is possible to combine two or more rooms for an assembly of the whole School. There are no specialist teaching rooms. All the senior girls attend a Housecraft Centre some distance from the School and*

have the use of an attractive Hall in St. George's School for dancing. The School has the help of a visiting pianist for dancing and a visiting teacher for Needlework. The girls go regularly to swimming but the playing fields on Woodhouse Moor are so far away that they are seldom used.

The premises are in urgent need of decoration. The walls of the classrooms, corridors and staircases are in a very dirty condition and much of the wall plaster is damaged. There are only five WCs but these are clean and regularly disinfected. Cloakroom and washing accommodation is inadequate and there is no hot water supply to the wash basins. The Staff room in the basement is cheerless and uncomfortable. A coke store behind the School is in a state of disrepair.

The desks in the junior classrooms are old, heavy and backless and cannot be moved to make the best possible use of the space in these rooms.

Ninety girls stay for the Mid-day Meal which is served in a room in the old part of St. George's School. Conditions are crowded, the room is cold and dismal and the walls are dirty and in need of repair. Although the physical conditions are not conducive to good standards, the meals are carefully conducted under supervision by the teachers.

The sink in the washing-up kitchen is small, the zinc covering on the draining boards is torn and dangerous, and the gas heater is faulty.

The Head Mistress was appointed to this School in September 1949, after previous experience as Head Mistress of two schools in Lancashire. In her previous posts she was responsible for younger children and she was free from class teaching. Her present school offers a different challenge: she is responsible for a class and for the teaching and direction of the work of the senior girls. So far this challenge had only been partially met, but she is most anxious for the welfare of the girls and the success of the School as a community. The girls are pleasant to meet; they are friendly and helpful and there is nothing unnatural in their courtesy to one another, to the Staff and to visitors.

In the view of the Head Mistress's previous experience, it is not surprising that the greatest development in the work of the School is to be found in the junior and transition classes. Even in these classes the development is of recent growth and it is early to assess it accurately. However, it is clear that as far as physical conditions have permitted, there had been a change from more formal class teaching. The work is developing in ways more natural to the children and more related to their interests. There is evidence of progress which is consistent with the girls' new enthusiasm, their greater understanding, and the encouragement given to them to respond according to their abilities. In the knowledge of the success of their work so far, and its *advantage to the girls, the teachers should be encouraged to go forward with confidence.*

The work of the senior girls is less convincing. Where their enthusiasm has been fired - in needlework, singing and dancing - they have responded well and have shown imagination, sensitive feeling and good taste. Good standards of presentation have been achieved in written work but the nature of the work does not call forth their best efforts: much of it is superficial. They are capable of something more then mechanical skill in reading, writing and in calculation. They would accept the challenge of work demanding more intensive study, wider reading and the power to think for themselves. They would welcome the opportunity to work independently and to develop further their own interests in Art, Music, Language and the outside world. In some respects the School is equipped to help the girls to go ahead on the above lines. It has a film projector, gramophone and wireless receiver and the ordinary tools are in good supply. The present Library, however, consists almost wholly of light fiction and will need to be supplemented to include the best in literature and more reference books.

Following the Inspection a meeting was held with the Head Mistress and Staff to review the recent progress in some aspects of the work of the School and to discuss the means whereby the work of the whole School might be directed more effectively towards the fuller development of the girls' powers.

Notes and References

1 Family Birth, Marriage and Death certificates.
2 Log Book in the Diocesan Archive - *St Anne's Junior Girls School:* 14 March 1923-21 July 1971.
3 *Ibid*
4 Lawson John., Silver Harold *A Social History of Education* Methuen & Co Ltd, London 1973
5 Finnegan Robert Diocesan Archives
6 Gaute JHH, Odell R *The Murders' Who's Who: 150 Years of Notorious Cases* Harrap, London 1980
7 *Ibid*
8 Reference in *St Anne's Junior Log Book* 16 November 1954 Chamber music for schools at Salem church - special transport was provided.
9 Leeds City Reference Library *Yorkshire Evening News* (on Microfilm) 23 March to June 1953.
10 *Ibid*
11 Official Programme of Events in Leeds, *Coronation of Her Most Gracious Majesty Queen Elizabeth II Second of June Nineteen Fifty Three.*
12 Leeds City Reference Library *Leeds Evening News* (on Microfilm) July to September 1953
13 Green S *Leeds Children's Day* Baron Publishing 1995
14 Log Book in the Diocesan Archive *St Anne's Junior Girls School:*14 March 1923 - 21 July 1971
15 Log Book in the Diocesan Archive. *St Anne's Junior Girls School:* 14 March 1923 - 21 July 1971
16 Official programme of Events in Leeds, *Coronation of Her Most Gracious Majesty Elizabeth II Second June Nineteen Fifty Three*
17 Log Book in the Diocesan Archive - *St Anne's Junior Girls School:* 14 March 1923 - 21 July 1971
18 Diocesan Archive- cutting of Jimmy Savile in *Yorkshire Evening Post*
19 Log Book *Ibid*
20 *Ibid*
21 *Ibid*
22 *Ibid*

Acknowledgements

I gratefully acknowledge the assistance given to me at the Leeds Diocesan Archives in St Mark's Avenue, particularly by Robert Finnegan, who lent me the photograph of the then Bishop Heenan and patiently answered my questions and produced old school records. Also thanks to Freda Matthews, of the Yorkshire Archeological Society, who when I mentioned my year at St Anne's, suggested it would be a good subject for my first attempt at writing. Thanks are also due to Miss Edna Bews for the use of some of her photographs.

11. ZIMMY'S: A GLIMPSE OF FACTORY LIFE IN A PRE-WAR CLOTHING FACTORY

by Isadore Pear

IN THE EARLY THIRTIES if you failed to win a scholarship, you were doomed to leave school at fourteen and become factory fodder. 'Teach him to learn a trade. It's better than nothing' was the stoical lament of disappointed parents; but the only trades open to us at that time, children of immigrant Jews, were either the wood trades, cabinet making and upholstery, cobblering or clothing. There was an effort of sorts to find me a job in an office. A local rent collector required a junior, so I was sent along for an interview with an introductory note from my teacher. The prospective employer glanced at it, and then glared down at me with a look that would have melted steel. He exposed his prejudice like a weapon. Then finally, in a voice so chilly it could have frozen ice-cream, he asked what church did I go to. Surprise, surprise, I was not offered the job! So as most of my family were employed in tailoring, there remained little doubt where I was destined to go.

The local tailoring trade in those days consisted of a few old established English owned firms such as John Barron's and Joseph Mays; and a little later a handful of major enterprises such as Burton's, manufacturing under the trademark *The Tailor of Taste*. They employed thousands of people in an immense factory complex in Hudson Road, Harehills, supplying hundreds of their own High Street shops. Another huge concern was Town Tailors whose slogan was *Weaver to Wearer, the Thirty Shilling Tailor* where one could purchase a suit made to measure for equivalent of £1.50 today. There were also quite a large number of medium sized factories, Hepworths in Claypit Lane, Ben Simons and J and M Harrison in Park Lane, Sumries in York Road, the Gloucester in or around Camp Road and many, many more far too numerous to mention. They in turn, by subcontracting to outworkers spawned hundreds of small independent workshops housed in cellars, front rooms and attics which employing thousands of people, often in deplorable conditions. In such places as these the trade was diversified into sections where jackets were made in one place, trousers in another, and waistcoats (or vests) somewhere else. Even these operations were

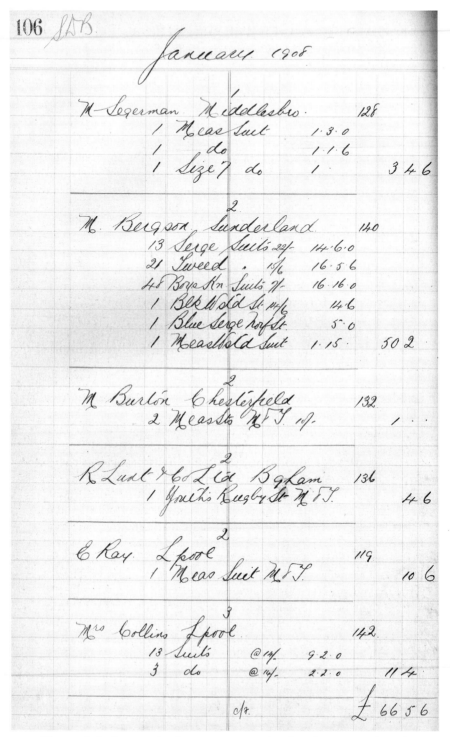

Figure 1. Ledger entries from 1906-1911 showing the supply of goods to the Burton's shops in Chesterfield and Mansfield. *Courtesy of Brian Zimmerman*

222 158

February 1909.

	Brought fd.	£.888 9 2	
M Collins L.pool. 26	182.		
6 Suits @16/-		£ 16 .	
Bunton. Mansfield 23	177		
1 Meas Norf St. N̄T̄	10.0		
1 „ fr Riding Brchs	3.6	13 6	
2 Blue Serge Meas St. 8/- 26	177.	16 .	
Geo Wilson S. land 24	180.		
6 Bk Vic fd v @6/-		1 16 .	
M Bergson. S. land 25	424		
1 Blue Vic Suit 12/6	186	12 6	
Bunton. C. field 26	177		
1 Bk West d Shooting C-Vest.		14 .	
Brown Son & Co. T. 26	165		
341 pr tros. Une 3/2	58.14.10		
2 Hampers @£1.	2. 0. 0	60 14 10	
G Brownson Ltd. Hyde 26	131		
47 Suits M v T 6/-		14 2 .	
Adee & Ryzer. Leeds 26	192		
11 Mens St. T̄ v T̄ 7/6	4. 2. 6		
2 Boys „ „ 6/-	12.0		
5 Brstrs „ 1/10	9. 2	5 . 3. 8	
	Card fd.	£ 977 17 8	

Figure 2. Ephraim
Zimmerman.
Courtesy of Brian Zimmerman

Figure 4. Hyman
(Hymy) Zimmerman.
Courtesy of Berenice Lipkin

Figure 3. Richard Isaac
Zimmerman.
Courtesy of Brian Zimmerman

Figure 5. Abraham
(Abe) Zimmerman.
Courtesy of Joe Manning

Figure 6. Harry Zimmerman.
Courtesy of Elaine Zimmerman

broken down still further, by sending half finished garments out to be buttonholed, and then finally out to yet another small outfit to be pressed off.

I started my working life in 1934 at the age of fourteen along with a few other boys from school in the cutting room at Zimmerman Brothers in Claypit Lane, one such medium-sized clothing factory of about 400 employees, both Jewish and non-Jewish. Two hundred were employed at Claypit Lane, and the remainder in St Anne's Street. The St Anne's factory was engaged solely in the production of trousers. The cutting room served both units. Overall the firm made all types of men's outerwear for the retail trade. It actually supplied Burton's when it only boasted two shops in Chesterfield and Mansfield (Figure 1).

Zimmy's was a self-contained factory where every stage of production was carried out under one roof. The factory was a family firm, owned by my uncle Ephraim and managed by cousins all much older than myself (Figure 2). My eldest cousin Dick was the Managing Director. He alone was accorded the respectful form of address of Mr Isaac, all the rest of the managerial staff, mostly Dick's brothers, were addressed casually by their first name. Dick is now ninety five years of age , active and, thank God, in good health. He is the oldest living Jewish clothing manufacturer in Leeds. He plays a regular round of golf, but only nine holes!; and is a more than average artist exhibiting and selling all for charity. A remarkable man (Figure 3). Hymy managed the coat room, Uncle Abe, Ephraim's brother was in charge of quality control; Harry, my immediate boss was the cutting room manager, whilst Joe looked after the office (Figures 4-

6). Bessie was a clerk. Two other young cousins Abe's sons Joe and David, worked in the coat room under the eagle eye of their father. They complained frequently about their inability to 'laik about' like the rest of us. But in the long run it paid dividends, as later David became a master craftsman in his own right and was a much sought after tailor by well known personalities of the time. Other non-family managerial staff consisted of Ted Williams, general administrator, Pinkie Zimmerman (no relation) controlled the trouser factory in St Anne's Street, Joe Cohen was the designer, Reg Barratt the pattern cutter and Donald Johnson and his wife Elsie, were in charge of packing and the stock room.

Figure 7. Shmuel Boruch Zimmerman.
Courtesy of Bessie Scholnick

My uncle was the eldest of a large family of Lithuanian Jews who had emigrated on his own at the tender age of sixteen in 1889. The rest of the family were to follow. My grandfather Shmuel Baruch Zimmerman and his daughter Jane (who was my mother) were the last of the family to arrive (Figure 7). Despite the language barrier, he dragged himself up from nothing; taking in out-work from John Barron's and Joseph Mays whose policy was to have work made outside by cheap immigrant labour, he sometimes worked through the night to fulfil orders. In fact, any work of a complicated or difficult nature was always farmed out. So it became a byword to all and sundry with the colloquialism *'Give it to the Sheenies. They'll sort it out'*.[1]

My starting wage was 2³/4d per hour in old money, or about ten shillings (50p) for a forty-eight hour week. This was a farthing more than the statutory minimum wage. A farthing in those days still had value. We were all paid slightly more than anywhere else, and this reflected favourably when compared to a man's wage of between £3.00 and £3.10 shillings (£3.50) depending upon his skill. Tailors were paid more than cutters, and good piece workers would earn more than either. Piece work meant being paid for a particular operation at an agreed price. The working conditions were relaxed, informal and friendly; far ahead of its time, although we had no

Figure 8. Isadore Pear aged 13.
Author's collection

canteen in the cutting room, and we snatched our tea breaks at the table where we worked. We had ample time, albeit unofficially, for lots of mischief and innocent fun. Nevertheless, anyone suspected of mean behaviour ran the risk of finding their coat pockets sewn up! However, in contrast to the stereotyped image of coarse factory folk, serious swearing was discouraged, especially when women and girls came into the room. So on one occasion after a squabble with another lad when I called him the worst word I knew, which reflected doubt as to his paternity, the manager, cousin Harry, made me apologise. The cutters themselves displayed a commendable degree of moral responsibility. If, when discussing something of an intimate or dubious nature, they saw me approaching, they would drop their voices and whisper 'Hark it, the kid's 'ere' (Figure 8). There was a union, the Tailor and Garment Workers, but membership was voluntary. However, it did not carry a very strong presence, and those people that did join, did so more for the social benefits such as sick pay when off ill, rather than opposition to working conditions. In fact, one non-Jewish employee, Walter, the foreman presser with an unpronounceable Polish name, actually had it changed to Zimmerman. There were no restrictions on talking whilst working, and we were freely permitted to chatter amongst ourselves. Provided we never 'knocked', that is persistent absenteeism, and we did our work, there were no other serious restrictions to speak of.

On turning up for work we were required to 'clock in' by punching the time clock, and if we were more than eight minutes late we were quartered (that is we lost a quarter of an hours pay). More than half an hour late without a convincing excuse meant facing being locked out. This was mandatory in all the big factories, but although it was part of the rules of employment here, it was never to my knowledge ever carried out, even though some of the excuses offered were so outrageous they could never have been believed. One young man slightly older than me, who left shortly after to join the police force, claimed he could not leave his dog because it was unwell. That was the first we ever heard that he had a dog, and nobody took the trouble to question it. The cutting room was an all male preserve of about thirty-five men, youths and boys. We were all paid on hourly rates. The cutting room was situated on the ground floor. It was a large rectangular room fitted with a number of long cutting tables, at least twelve to twenty feet long and thirty inches wide. There were also smaller tables for ancillary work. The table tops had to be frequently replaced as they became worn from sliding cloths. The walls were surrounded by floor to ceiling fixtures for storing cloth. The only machines were the band knife, this was a large circular saw with a twelve inch exposed blade, used for cutting through thick layers of cloth, and several smaller hand machines Eastman cutters for cutting the various interlinings which were to be sewn into the clothes. The former was handled only by a highly skilled operative; the latter by youngsters like myself. Some time later children under sixteen were forbidden from using any type of power machines. By contrast to the remainder of the factory, the ambience of the cutting room remained tranquil and serene; pierced only by the drone of the band knife, the clicking of the hand shears and the comfortable hum of conversation. Elsewhere, by comparison, was like bedlam with constant noise from the machines and the insidious hiss of steam from the battery of presses in the finishing department. A minor, but integral part of the production process was the disposal of 'clips'. These were the tiny bits of cloth left after cutting out. They were bagged in sacks and collected periodically by a rag merchant who resorted and sold them to woollen mills where once again they were woven back into cloth.

Being the most junior member of the cutting room, part of my job entailed running errands and carrying messages to other departments, so I quickly became acquainted with other young folk, including of course, girls! An errand to the trousers room was a particular delight and often search parties were sent out to see if I had emigrated. Surreptitious meetings were hastily arranged in the stock room, another quiet part of the factory, where one could easily hide between the huge piles of cloth, or between the completed rows of hung garments waiting to be despatched. But woe-betide you if you were caught by Donald. He showed no compunction in throwing you out of his domain. But that was the end of the matter; no malice and no tales. Looking back we were a lively bunch of kids, and in the prevailing relaxed atmosphere we needed some handling. By the very nature of the job it became repetitive and boring carrying out each process, chopping and trimming (the technical terms for cutting out) and preparing interlinings for previously cut out cloth waiting to be made up over and over again, day in and day out. Small wonder, as juniors, we sought every opportunity to find diversion to give vent to our high spirits by running errands which provided legitimate reason to leave one's table. One such particular errand eagerly anticipated on a hot day, was the one of going out for a Vantas drink. This was a proprietary drink sold loose from a dispenser, popular at that time. At the side of the factory in Back Grove Terrace there was a tiny grocery shop come general store which stocked everything from boot laces to elephants. There were goods on shelves, on the floor and on the counter, and, for good measure hardware items such as brushes and buckets hung from the ceiling. It also provided refreshments. For a halfpenny, providing you brought your own mug, you had it filled up with this cool fizzy drink. You could choose whatever flavour you liked, but had to be content with whatever flavour they had, which was generally Sarsparella. So when the cutters sent us out we pleaded to have it full to overflowing and then enjoyed a liberal sample ourselves. Before returning we swished the mug around, thus producing a sparkling froth and nicely concealing the missing measure. Nobody was fooled, but we were all happy.

Women and girls dominated the sewing machines. They too started on hourly rates whilst learning, but could opt to go on to piece work once they became proficient. Leeds, being the largest clothing centre in the North, attracted many experienced hands seeking work, and in some instances, husbands! Zimmy's, employing quite a large contingent of single girls from Glasgow, provided an ideal meeting place for proposed matrimonial matches. Inevitably one such marriage involved a Jewish girl and a Gentile boy, which in those days was severely discouraged. This ignited a great deal of vigorous controversy from both Jewish and non-Jewish sources, and although she was under no compulsion to do so, the girl in question left. The marriage however, proved successful and happy, and in later years I got to know them and their daughter Brenda very well.

As Zimmy's was a privately owned Jewish concern, and my uncle a devout Jew, legislation permitted the factory to operate on a

Sunday instead of Saturday, the Jewish Shabbat, the holy day of rest. This was quite commonplace at the time amongst other Jewish owned establishments. Attendance for the non-Jewish workers was of course optional. So we had Saturdays off, but worked three hours on Sunday morning instead. It also enabled Jewish customers to replenish stocks. One such customer, Mr I Cohen who was in business in Doncaster, but who lived in Leeds, usually came buying accompanied by his wife and younger daughter. Whilst they were engaged, his daughter and I were similarly engaged flirting. Several years later she became my wife. The rest of the week we worked Monday to Thursday from 8.00am to 6.00pm or 7.00pm depending upon how busy we were. On Friday we worked from 8.00am to one hour before sundown in winter, prior to the onset of Shabbat; in summer we worked until 6.00pm.

When we were busy we worked overtime until 9.30pm, but when we were slack in the height of summer we were laid off and had to sign on for three days unemployment benefit at the labour exchange. Unfortunately this inevitably proved a great burden for the family man. However a benign and generous management discreetly helped out when any undue hardship occurred. But to all the 'youngsters' like me with little or no responsibilities, the slack time was like manna from heaven, a God-send. We were too young to sign on as eighteen was the minimum age before we could draw benefit, so we were allowed to work until midday and then we were off like greyhounds, dashing away to enjoy our freedom at Roundhay Park open air pool. Shortly after this further legislation prohibited children under eighteen years from working longer than forty four hours, so that put an end to the long overtime.

A service I remember well, common to the trade, was that of 'funerals'. Not the ones subscribed to an undertaker, but a euphemism we used to characterise very urgent orders. The whole factory 'mucked in' trying to beat the previous record. Generally, from receiving one such order on the phone, a made-to-measure suit could be completed and despatched within three hours. And whilst on such a melancholy subject of funerals, another expression of the trade which comes to mind was that one of 'kills'. This was the overall term used to describe a calamity, whereby goods were irretrievably damaged during the process of being made up. Inquests were taboo. They necessarily took up valuable time without establishing anything other than it was an accident. Management never laid blame, nor sought excuses, it merely wanted to ensure that whatever had occurred would never happen again. That was company policy. Deliberate vandalism of course, earned instant dismissal. In some factories a damage fund of one penny per head was levied on the work force to pay for such mishaps, but never, to my knowledge, at Zimmy's.

After a couple of years, in 1936, I was promoted up the ladder. As a stock cutter, earning more money and receiving holidays with pay, running errands was a thing of the past. I felt like a millionaire, on top of the world. But there were other sinister influences at work. Gambling. All the cutters backed horses. Every day they made bets before coming in to work. So I joined them, and despite my new found affluence, by Wednesday or Thursday I was 'skint'. Then the penny dropped. Rather than accept the odds, why not lay them? So I became a bookmaker. My office was the table at which I worked. Initially I opened a book solely for the cutting room, accepting bets from 1d to 3d in old money. It did so well that I extended my territory to the other departments, recruiting agents from my many friends at one shilling (5p) in the £1 commission. Work virtually stopped as everybody was engrossed in making bets. After four days I was £7 in front, but on the fifth, disaster! Four favourites won and I lost £3. But that was not the only thing I lost, I almost lost my job! Of course the whole concept was impossible and I had to stop, but I learned a valuable lesson, never to back horses, and indeed, not to gamble at all!

In the same year, 1936, my aunt, Ephraim's wife, died. In Judaism it is prescribed that following the death of a relative, the next of kin observe the ritual of saying a special memorial prayer, the Kaddish, three times a day for eleven months in their memory. A minimum quorum of ten men is required. So every lunch time we held a short service for this purpose. One day, a regular and familiar traveller wandered in unannounced during our devotions, and beat a hasty and apologetic retreat for disturbing what he was thought was a board meeting!

The day war was declared was Sunday 3 September at 11.00am. I remember it clearly as I was at work. When the announcement came over the radio (we called it the wireless then), the whole factory came to a standstill. The silence was deafening. It took several minutes before returning to normal. Everybody held an opinion and had something to say. I remember my uncle , who had become an arch patriot saying in 'Yinglish' (a mongrel form of Yiddish and English) *'Nu vi den mir daf gain fighten'* (It is our duty to go and fight). I was called up shortly afterwards, as were all the boys in the cutting room, and a chapter of my life closed. I had little realised before, how well I had been cocooned (Figure 9).

Zimmerman Brothers first came into existence in the early 1900s

Figure 9. Isador Pear aged 17.
Author's collection

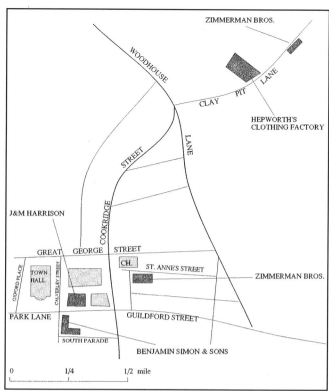

Figure 10. Map showing locations of the clothing factories.
Map redrawn from Ordnance Survey 1:2500 1908 by David Wycherley

in Telephone Building situated in Cross Stamford Street, Newtown. From there it moved to Claypit Lane, occupying first one floor, then two, and eventually the whole building. A compulsory purchase order for road widening issued by the local authority dictated the next move round the corner to Grove Terrace (Figure 10). The St Anne's Street factory was opened in 1936 and closed in the early 1950s. Finally, it moved yet again by a further compulsory purchase order from Grove Terrace to a modern, purpose built factory in

Figure 11. Zimmerman's purpose built factory on Meanwood Road.
Author's collection

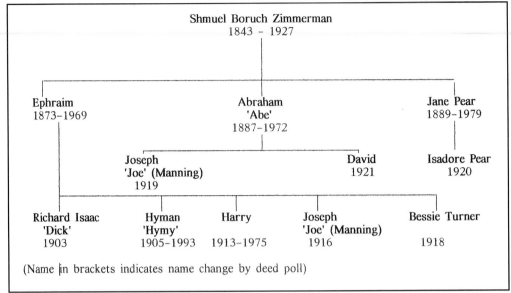

Figure 12. Zimmerman family tree.

Meanwood Road, and in 1970, after almost seventy years the business was sold to a Manchester conglomerate (Figure 11). However, the family still retain a single, slender link with the trade as Brian, Isaac's son and Ephraim's grandson, continues to operate an import export agency concerned primarily with the importation of foreign clothing (Figure 12). Ironically, it was the import of foreign clothing which killed the local clothing trade. Of the other factories mentioned earlier, all of them are long since gone with the exception of Burton's which has survived, but in a totally different guise from its original conception.

Notes and Reference

1 'Sheenies', a derogatory reference to the Jews

Acknowledgements

I am deeply grateful to Brian Zimmerman for the generous loan of the firm's ledgers. I also extend a heartfelt thank you to all my relatives for the use of their precious photographs:Berenice Lipkin, Joseph Manning (Abe's son), Bessie Scholnick, Brian Zimmerman and Elaine Zimmerman. And finally, for her patience, encouragement and help, I am sure over and above her normal professional duty, my editor Lynne Stevenson Tate. Bless you all!

12. THE FIRST UNION DISPUTE WITH THE AIRE & CALDER NAVIGATION COMPANY, LEEDS– DURING THE WINTER OF 1891-1892

by William Scott

THE AIRE & CALDER NAVIGATION COMPANY (A&CN) had its origin in the *Improvement Act* of 1699 which was intended to allow the passage of barges capable of carrying fifteen tons of cargo (an incredible amount when compared with the then movements by cart on ill-maintained and badly rutted roadways) to reach Leeds along the river Aire and Wakefield, by way of the river Calder - the confluence being near Castleford. So-called 'Undertakers' were appointed to carry out the work together with Commissioners and Trustees.

Aimed at the lucrative West Riding cloth trade of both towns the embryonic company transformed itself over the succeeding years into one of the most powerful and influential companies in Yorkshire; it was pre-eminent among the Canal and Barge companies which emerged from the 'Canal Mania' of the late eighteenth century.

By 1891 the population of Leeds and its townships comprised 367,000 souls. The Industrial Revolution and urbanisation programmes of the early and mid-nineteenth century resulted, by

Figure 1. Leeds Lock, c1895. Lock keepers were important officials of the Navigation. Apart from ensuring thier locks were kept tidy and clear of debris they had to be agile enough to pass flyboats through at speed. They also were responsible for charging and collecting toll money from passing cargo.

1891, in a population some nineteen percent greater than only ten years previously and a massive forty two percent increase from 1871. That substantial and continuing growth was allied to, and the main reason for, the increasing importance of Leeds as an industrial town. This in turn led to an ever growing demand for land, houses, food and foodstuffs, clothes and fuel to maintain that rate of expansion.

The towns and villages through which the Aire & Calder, the Calder & Hebble, and Bradford Canals passed, reflected similar growth but it was Leeds which emerged as the dynamic industrial centre. Its prosperity was based on the clothing trade; with its great White and Coloured Cloth Halls and the thriving Cloth Market on Leeds Bridge, Leeds was famous throughout the country and on the continent for the quality and quantity of its cloth. The A&CN sought to exploit that and, by 1891, the company had an influence well beyond Yorkshire and its energy and initiatives in the transport field were such that employment by the Company was much sought after (Figures 1,2 & 3)

A large part of the company's barge fleet comprised of so-called 'Fly Boats' which ran an express service to strict timetables and took precedence over other craft navigating the canals, with the additional privilege of being allowed to pass through locks at night, a concession denied other craft. The Fly boats displayed prominent distinguishing markings in order that their importance was recognised. Due to their higher costs (for example they required more frequent changes of towing horses or the expensive steam tugs) the goods that they carried commanded higher rates and tolls. Accordingly Fly boat crews were treated with a measure of respect and their occupation

Figure 2. Barge under sail. Humber c1880. Sails were taken down at the entrance to the canal system at Goole, the barge then being towed to Leeds or other West Riding towns by horse or steam tug.

Figure 3. Barges awaiting cargo. Leeds c1895. Although giving an appearance of confusion, the barges were loaded in strict rotation and under the supervision of cargo checkers.

attracted a generally higher calibre and more literate class with an attendant glamour denied their more mundane colleagues. (Figure 4)

The introduction of Fly boats, in Yorkshire, was a response to the increasing competition from the scheduled steam packet service on the River Ouse, and later, when the railway companies became a growing threat, the numbers of Fly boats in service increased dramatically and was allied to expansive improvements in the canal infrastructure. The A&CN operated their own Fly boats as early as 1821, running between Leeds and Selby and leaving Leeds each evening to reach Selby the following morning. Although horses continued to be used well into the 1890s, from around 1831 the Fly boats were increasingly being towed by steam tugs, with the added advantage of the tugs themselves carrying highly profitable cargos.

Fly boats loaded and discharged their various goods at intermediate points along the canal system. For example, between Leeds and Goole, a navigation distance of thirty four miles, there were thirty separate wharves, eight mills, eleven coal mines and staithes, four chemical works, five glass and bottling works, two copper works, two lime kilns, two forges and three potteries, all of which took in and sent out their materials by barge. By far the

Figure 4. Boatmen, c1905. A splendid photograph of canal boatmen. Their apparel is little changed from that worn some 20 years earlier (see caption 7).

Figure 5. Coal Staithes, Leeds, late 1890's. Coal was a prime cargo and consequently loading needed to be fast and efficient. Steam cranes were used extensively, lifting over a ton each time into the barge loading chute.

Figure 6. Discharging wool, Leeds c1900. Wool was an important cargo both in volume and revenue terms. The Leeds Town warehouse had been a major wool store since the mid 18th century.

biggest single commodity moved, in volume terms, was coal both for domestic and burgeoning industrial markets. Demand for coal was insatiable as it became the predominant energy source; indeed the rapid replacement of water power to steam and coke smelting ensured a valuable and increasing income to the canal and railway companies (Figures 5-6).

The growing market for factory-made textiles (as opposed to home produced clothes) also provided a rich source of income for the Navigation. Substantial amounts of bales of wool from the Empire were discharged overside at Hull into barges for transport to Wakefield, Leeds, Halifax and Bradford. Building bricks, perhaps surprisingly, were another very important cargo. The rapid and intensive spread of dwellings in the main towns, particularly in places like Leeds, demanded massive supplies of building materials and barge transport combined the best form of unit quantity, speed and cost. Wheat, barley and grain was moved in huge quantities as were cocoa, logs, salt, iron ores and powders that formed part of the myriad types of commodities carried on the canal. In an age without real refrigeration, Fly boats were extensively used to carry perishable goods; their speed and strict timetables making them ideal for this.

The operation and management of such a large company was carried out by District Agents; each area was controlled by what one would term today an Area Manager who in turn derived his authority from the General Manager in Leeds. In 1891 the General Manager was the redoubtable and well known engineer, William Hammond Bartholomew. Mr Bartholomew epitomised the Victorian work ethic. He had been both Engineer and General Manager of the A&CN since 1875; in 1890 he was fifty nine years old and had already served the company over the past thirty nine years! This remarkable man was to continue in the company's service for a further twenty eight years and, though he reported to his board of directors, William Bartholomew was, in effect, the company.

His father, Thomas, had been appointed Resident Engineer of the A&CN in 1826 and his uncle, Charles, was Engineer to the River Don Navigation (the forerunners of the Sheffield & South Yorkshire

Figure 7. Compartment Boat Hoist, Goole, c1890. Bartholomew's innovative direct barge loading system. The compartment boats ('Tom puddings') were loaded on rail tracks within the colliery, hauled into the water towed along the canal to Goole hoist, lifted some 30ft (9m) when the coal was tipped through a chute directly into the ship.

Figure 8. Boatmen and families, Leeds c1875. Most general cargo barges (unlike flyboats) had the Captains (and on occasions the Mates) family on board. Education of the children was of necessity intermittent depending where the barges were laying up; the wives not only cooked, sewed and painted but on occasions also towed the barges over short sections unfit for horses.

Navigation Company) so it was only natural that William would join the A&CN when he was twenty.

Bartholomew was not only to become widely known and respected within the company and region but his inventive genius made his name familiar outside the north of England. Twenty eight years earlier and in order to compete with the railways, he patented designs for the so-called 'Compartment' Boats (later to become known as 'Tom Puddings') and lifting hoists at Goole which, by lifting the entire boat for discharging directly into ship, revolutionised the carrying trade on the canal and was the envy of other canal companies. His memorial lies in the fact that his system at Goole continued without undue change until 1983 and was replicated in the present coal discharging system at Ferrybridge Power Station (Figure 7). His Agents worked hard and assiduously and bearing in mind the time taken in travelling around their areas (by foot, carriage, barge or train) they were very efficient. Most had worked, or would work, all their lives for the company; they were not only completely familiar with all aspects of the canal but were, of necessity, close to their boatmen and understood, if they did not always share, their hardworking and precarious lives.

In the Autumn of 1889 a deputation of Fly boat Captains met the Leeds Agent, John Marston, to air their festering grievance over pay. Due to a dip in trade some five years earlier the A&CN had reduced their employees wages by ten per cent; trade had subsequently improved and the Captains understandably wanted that percentage re-instated. Their spokesmen, John Brooks, told the Agent that that week his earnings, in a busy seven day working week, had been 38s 6d (£1.95) though his average earnings were 34s 8d (£1.73) a week.[1]

To put their wages into perspective they need comparison with the average cost of living for a family of two adults and three to four children at the time. A comprehensive survey of 1900 dealing with regional and city costs showed that prices had actually fallen by one percent since 1892.[2] Even allowing for that the survey suggested the minimum requirement for food and heating (coals) for a family was 24s 3d (£1.21) per week. Additionally a typical rent of a four room 'back to back' house in Leeds was between four shillings (20p) and five shillings (25p) each week. Compared with a barge captain's average wage, this left 9s 9d (52p) weekly for clothing and footware, any medical costs, such little education as could be afforded and any drink and tobacco. Obviously, in dire hardship, the food intake and expenditure on clothes and shoes would be drastically reduced but at a social and emotional cost to the family which is difficult now to appreciate. (Figure 8 & 9)

Though the Leeds Agent had promised to look into the men's grievance it was not until June of the following year that he in fact brought up the matter with his General Manager. A letter had been received from the General Laborers[sic] Dock & Riverside Union in Hull stating that unless the Fly boatmen joined the union the company's barges would not be handled in the port. As a large amount of goods were loaded and discharged in Hull the A&CN pressed their men to join to protect trade, at a cost to the men of 5s (25p) joining fee and 2d (1p) per week thereafter! The Leeds Agent, at that time, mentioned the previous year's meeting with the men over wages.

Between June and December of 1890 several meetings took place between men and management, presided over by Mr Bartholomew, but without any concessions from the company. The situation was exacerbated by the management issuing, on Christmas Eve, notices to the effect that due to the hard frost the men would be laid off (without pay of course) until the weather and therefore trade improved. The winter of 1890-91 was severe; ice and fog, those twin problems for canals, together with driving snow stopped barge transport for long periods. The issuing of 'lay-off' notices was common practice and underlined the precarious nature of the men's employment. The A&CN were considered good employers but their philosophy was a simple one: if the revenue was stopped then so must the costs. The volatile effects of trade impacted quickly on employment; if for example coal movements were reduced for several weeks then boats, and men, were laid off. It was difficult if not impossible for men to set anything aside from their earnings to cushion the effects of such lay-offs. No State help was available and destitution was 'corrected' by the Workhouse!

The resentment of the boatmen to the lack of progress over their wage claim continued unabated. That increasing numbers had joined the union is evident by the fact that a meeting with the union had been agreed by the A&CN board at the monthly meeting in February 1891 and it was then apparently accepted by the company that the union was the negotiating body on behalf of the men. Little is known of the union agents concerned, a Mr Maloney and Mr Clayton other than both had appeared to play a prominent part with Hull Port and had been charged with pressing the boatmen's claim.

Mr Bartholomew, under the direction of the A&CN board (who had finally woken to the fact that they may have a difficult dispute on their hands) met the union in Hull in March 1891. Whilst granting a small concession as regards the payment of overtime when discharging or loading craft in Hull or Goole, he resisted the

Figure 9. Horse drawn barge, Leeds and Liverpool canal, Leeds 1905.

increasing pressure for a seven and a half percent wage increase. He
told the meeting he would be considering the claim and would report
to his board within 'a month or six weeks'.[1] His intention, made plain
to the board subsequently, was to concede two and a half percent
rather than the full seven and a half percent and he was confident
that that would not only satisfy the men but would allow him to get
further concessions from them by way of 'productivity'. He
calculated that the overtime cost would be £300 annually with the
two and a half percent in wages costing a further £400. To pay for
that and in advance of any agreement with the union he increased the
grain trade traffic by 5d (2p) per ton immediately. That, he
considered, would accrue £1100 per annum. For the sake therefore
of a further £400 annually he intended to call the union's bluff

Negotiations in those days had not the same imperative as now and
despite the board's unease they had more important matters to deal
with. Accordingly it was not until late November that a second
formal meeting with the union took place. This time however the
unions called in their big guns: Mr Ben Tillett headed the union
team. His appearance on the scene is interesting. Aged thirty one at
the time and a committed socialist as well as a trade union leader he
was described in newspapers at the time as an 'Agitator'. His rapid
rise in trade union circles and in the future Labour Party was some
way off but already by 1891 he was well known in trade disputes and
was recognised as a hard negotiator. His manipulation of the Tilbury
Docks stoppage three years earlier and his *No Work Manifesto* - a call
for a General Strike within the London Docks - had made him well
known. An evidently ambitious man who nonetheless cared
passionately for working people he had become General Secretary of
the so-called Tea Operatives & General Labourers Association later
the Dock, Wharf, Riverside and General Labourers Union in 1887;
that evolved into the Transport & General Workers Union after 1921.

His militant socialist views were well known by 1891 and his
presence in a dispute not only strengthened the union negotiators
but heartened the men on whose behalf he was acting. His dictum
was simple:

> *Once a Union had a fair following in a given place of work and
> enjoyed some recognition by the Employer, it could bring social
> pressure to bear on those still outside.*[3]

Union membership was growing and was perceived as an insidious
and real threat to commerce. By 1891 some five percent of the so-
called 'occupied' population of one million six hundred thousand

were members of a union; of those some sixty thousand were in transport related work.

While Ben Tillett was a delegate to the Trade Union Congress for three years from 1892 and served on the Executive of the Labour Party in 1901 he made enemies both within and outside the movement. A Member of Parliament towards the end of the First World War (and until 1931) none of his detractors however could fault his idealism and achievements for his fellow men. In a rather acerberic assessment, his presence and vision were summed up by William Collinson in his pamphlet *The Apostle of Free Labour* in 1913 as:

> *...a Demagogue with the taste of a sybarite; a voluptuary with the hide of an Agitator...he never knew how to labour and to wait. Ever grasping at the present shadow of fleeting popularity he lost the substance of future greatness.*[4]

Despite that view, Mr Tillett must have been one of the great Victorian characters and his presence in Leeds on a dark noisome November day must have given the Aire & Calder managers some anxiety. It is a pity that his discussions and asides with Mr Bartholomew, an equally hard headed and pragmatic Victorian, were not recorded.

Perhaps due to the presence of Ben Tillett or to a growing realisation that unless some concession was made a strike appeared inevitable, Bartholomew offered a further two and a half percent but with the proviso that it would be paid on a 'rate per ton' basis i.e. as a bonus and in any event would be on a three months trial. While the unions promised to put the offer to the men they were in little doubt as to the outcome. Bartholomew's proposed wage increase based on

Figure 10. Barges laying off Warehouse Hill, Leeds c1920.

payment for each ton carried was bound to be rejected as he must have expected. Both the men and union were vehemently opposed to a system so dependent on the whims of time, tide and weather and the type of cargo carried.

Events moved swiftly. With a view to by-passing the union, Bartholomew made arrangements for a mass meeting to be held in Goole in the company's time and at its expense, on the fifteenth of December. Goole was an important trading centre for the A&CN; it had been built up and developed by the company from a few dwellings within remote areas of land largely reclaimed from the estuary in 1826 and appointed a United Kingdom port in 1828. By the 1880s the port had been consolidated and extended primarily to service the company in enhancing the carrying trade on the Aire & Calder. In fact William Bartholomew, in addition to his executive role with the company proper, had been appointed General Manager of the Goole Steam Shipping Company in 1880. His influence in Goole was widespread and no doubt he hoped to capitalise on that in choosing 'Goole Mission Hall' for a mass meeting. Virtually the whole of Goole's working population were employed directly or indirectly by the company and the effects of a long strike on the inhabitants would be catastrophic. At the same time, Goole port's importance to the the company exceeded that of Hull; from 1892 until the outbreak of the First World War the port enjoyed unrivalled prosperity, with thousands of tons of baled wool from Australia, New Zealand and South America coming through the port and along the Aire & Calder to the burgeoning mills of Bradford. The supply and carrying of coal was inexhaustible as was quantities of sugar from the West Indies and Africa, grain from Canada and Baltic timber.

The meeting in *Goole Mission Hall* on the 15 December 1891 was held in an atmosphere of belligerence on the men's part and apprehension on the company's. The Goole Agent, a Mr Potts, stationed himself outside the hall and handed each man going in a broadsheet explaining the company's proposals. Unfortunately for the company, it all backfired. The meeting, in some disorder 'loudly called' for their union officials to attend and a messenger was sent out for them. It was noted that the officials, Messrs Clayton and Maloney 'entered the room amidst loud and prolonged cheering'.[2]

The company's meeting was turned on its head and became simply a strike issue; of the one hundred and twelve men in attendance (out of a boat strength of one hundred and forty two - the others were on essential navigation duties - one hundred and eight voted for an all out strike.

On being advised of the outcome Mr Bartholomew made a last

attempt to change the union's stance. Four days later he met the union representatives in the company's boardroom in Leeds (paying their expenses from Hull) when, accompanied by three of his senior agents, he re-iterated at some length the company's offer and general proposals. His endeavours were unsuccessful. The union flatly rejected any cargo based system and demanded an immediate two and a half percent wage increase if they were to call off the strike. As one would expect given the stakes, it was a long and sometimes acrimonious discussion and finally Bartholomew told the union that the company could not and would not make further concessions. A strike notice, to begin on Christmas Eve, was then handed to the general Manager; the union gave instructions to their members to lay up craft 'wherever they may be at 6.00pm on 24 December' and the management hastily telegraphed their customers with details of the situation in an attempt to divert cargos. The confrontation that no one wanted nor imagined had actually arrived!

The men left their boats on Christmas Eve 1891, when they were each paid wages due. The dense fog which prevailed on that day (and had for some days previously) made it difficult to get the barges to safe moorings before the crews left; eventually that was accomplished just before midnight. Apart from any residual cargo in the craft the barges contained general working stores which had to be individually accounted for (Figure 10). There were some eighty five separate items, ranging from tow ropes to marlin spikes, from scuttles to oil lamps and any missing items would be charged to the men. Additionally, stabling and forage for over a hundred tow horses had to be dealt with. Each horse consumed around a quarter of a ton of feedstuff each week which had to be prepared and moved to assembly areas and it was no small task, in bitter foggy weather, to get everything in place.

One hundred and seventy eight men - eighty nine barge captains with the same number of mates - out of one hundred and ninety two skilled men came out on strike. A further eighty two men (dock labourers, draymen, 'horse' marines and some clerks) were as a consequence thrown out of work.

The strike lasted for seven weeks, from Christmas Eve 1891 until 5 February 1892 during one of the hardest winters for some years. While the company maintained some little trading from Goole using hired in craft (so-called 'bye-traders') albeit with difficulty - there was sporadic stone throwing and attempts at general intimidation - the lucrative Hull trade had to be switched to the railway companies who were of course only too anxious to help. (Figure 11 & 12)

Figure 11. Hull port 1905. Barges under sail with cargo for Leeds. The fast flowing Humber between Hull and Goole tested the endurance of boatmen. Sails could be split or torn in the fierce winds making navigation hazardous and the 4 to 5 hour journey, especially in winter and in ice or fog, demanded a concentration and dedication unimagined today.

The union paid the married strikers ten shillings (50p) per week but increasingly the men's determination to continue the strike weakened. In an internal note to Mr Bartholomew the Leeds Agent reported, some two weeks into the strike, that he had met Mr Maloney of the union when the latter had been paying strike pay at Leeds Bridge; on enquiring as to when he expected the strike to last Maloney said he had expected Ben Tillet 'to have settled the matter before now' and that had it been left to him he would have approached the company 'had he not thought it would have been seen as a weakness'.[5]

Figure 12. Barge striking sail. Old Harbour, Hull. 1903. The dismantling of masts when entering port or into the canal required some strength; little mechanical handling was available and striking sail at the same time as keeping the barge's 'head' up demonstrated the sheer skill of the Aire and Calder boatmen. Sail continued intermittently into the 1930s.

The strike cost the company some £3000 in direct expenditure, many thousands of pounds in lost revenue and a serious loss of trade to the railways which took a considerable time to recover. It cost the men far more. Their families were almost destitute and their futures uncertain. Six months after the strike ended the company was employing only half the numbers in work before. The management prepared a list of all their former employees

> *showing their general character and antecedents so that only the most suitable men may be selected as Captains and Mates when the strike is over.* [6]

So ended the first official union strike on the waterways. But who gained?

An extract from a memorandum William Bartholomew sent to his directors in Leeds on 8 February 1892 may give a clue:

> *Gentlemen, On the 3rd.instant the Hull Secretary of the Union telegraphed me that the Strike was at an end. The Boats will therefore be gradually put into commission as circumstances require. The men have, it will be seen, given way practically unconditionally (and) the advantages reaped by the Navigation therefrom may be stated to be as follows:*
>
> *A saving (upon the demands of the men) of at least £400 per annum in wages. An arrangement by which losses and damages are likely to be reduced An amended form of Agreement with the men which embraces more and is more binding than the former Agreement And, what is perhaps the most important, better discipline it is thought, has been secured; the men in consequence of their repeated demands for increased wages and less work, having become very difficult to control.* [7]

Notes and References

1 Aire & Calder Navigation.Strike of Fly Boatmen 1891 & 1892. Minutes and memorandum. Authors possession.
2 Cost of living of the working classes Board of Trade enquiry into Working Class Rents and retail prices together with rates of wages in certain occupations *Parliamentary Report*:HMSO.1905.
The Apostle of Free Labour William Collinson. 1913.

CONTRIBUTORS

Lynne Stevenson Tate was born in Bradford, brought up in Pudsey, has lived in Farsley since 1970. She worked as a bookseller in Leeds from 1971-98 and now works as a retail manager for Imperial Cancer Research Fund. A life long interest in history resulted in a BA Honours from the Open University in 1995, whilst working full time. She is married to Michael and they are both active in their local church. Lynne is the editor of *Aspects of Leeds 1* and *2*. She also undertakes freelance editorial work and has worked, and is working with a number of authors in the production of their biographies.

1. LEEDS UNITED: THE BREAKTHROUGH SEASON 1964-5

David Saffer is Leeds born and has followed Leeds United since 1968. Educated at Roundhay High School, he graduated in 1985 with an honours degree in Business Studies. After seven years selling computers in 'the smoke', relocation bought him back to Leeds. Today he is a director at Second Byte City Limited and has written two books with Howard Dapin, *Leeds United Cup Kings* 1972, and *Images of Sport: Leeds United*. He met his wife Deborah while studying, they married in 1986 and have three children, Daniella, Abigail and Jake.

Howard L. Dapin, a solicitor, is Leeds born and was educated at Leeds Grammar School. He obtained his Law degree at Manchester University, graduating in 1981. Spent much of his student days amongst away fans at both Old Trafford and Maine Road. On returning to Leeds married Benita. They have two daughters, Sophie and Jade, who have no interest in football whatsoever. He is now a partner in the national law firm Irwin Mitchell, and regularly watches Leeds as he has done since 1966.

2. VARITETY SPELLS ENTERTAINMENT: THE CINEMA LIFE OF CLUADE H WHINCUP

Moving to Leeds in 1976, **Robert Preedy** was fascinated by the number of former cinema buildings still standing in the city. This interest led to his first book in 1980, *Leeds Cinemas Remembered*. Since then he has written and published a further nine books including two recent ones about the UK history of Roller Coasters. Robert has also branched out into running his own cinemas. The first, the Castle Cinema, Pickering from 1984 to 1992 and since thn the Wetherby Film Theatre which he reopened in 1994 after thirty years closure as a cinema. His parallel career in broadcasting started with BBC TV and radio in London. Joining Yorkshire Television in 1976 he has been a cameraman, sound technician, researcher, promotions producer and continuity announcer. He has also broadcast with Radio Aire, Magic 828 and is currently heard on BBC local radio across the north with an American County Music show. The early history of radio and TV in Leeds is his current research project. Robert has a 12 year old son who loves running the Wetherby cinema. Robert also contributed an article in *Aspects of Leeds 1*

3. THOSE JAW BONES

William Banks was born in Rothwell in 1909. He was married and was the father of six children, five boys and girl, one of whom died. William was involved in pit life for over fifty years and during these years became active politically and held a number of senior positions. Throughout his life William was active in many aspects of Rothwell life and a district councillor for sixteen years. Further details can be found in

Who's Who. William had been long active in the Rothwell Local History Society and was for a number of years its secretary. William died on 26 December 1998, whilsts this book was in production.

4. GROWING UP IN NEW LEEDS

Kathleen Gurney was born in Leeds in 1920 and, after getting a job as a secretary in an advertising agency, moved between the North and the South of England before returning to Leeds at the outbreak of the Second World War. From 1942-46 she served in the WAAF. After demobilisation she took an Emergency Teacher training course and taught Art and English. She became interested in social and family history and joined the Yorkshire Archaelogical Society in 1973. She edited their magazine for a while and has carried out research for other members. Kathleen spends one morning a week doing voluntary work for the YAS archive and is currently engaged on the compilation of a wills index.

5. HUNSLET IN THE EIGHTEENTH CENTURY

John Goodchild is a native of Wakefield and was educated at the Grammar School there. He has been active in local historical research since about the age of thirteen, and is the author of over 140 books and published essays on aspects of the history of the West Riding. He was founder-curator of Cusworth Hall Museum and subsequently Archivist to Wakefield MDC; in his retirement he runs a Local History Study Centre which houses his immense collection of manuscripts and research materials, and which is open to use, free of charge, by appointment. Mr Goodchild holds an honorary M Univ from the Open University, awarded for academic and scholarly distinction and for public services. He is a regular contributor to the Aspects series. Outside historical research, his interests lie in Freemasonry and in

Unitarianism - and his dog. He has contributed to a number of 'Aspects' titles, including *Aspects of Leeds 1*.

6. POOR BUT HAPPY: HOLBECK IN THE THIRTIES

Ray Dobson was born in Leeds. After attending Ingram Road School in Holbeck, he left at age fourteen to take up office work as a junior insurance clerk. He left to complete two years National Service in the Royal Navy, and returned to the insurance industry. In 1958 he qualified as an Associate of the Chartered institute. After retiring he decided to pursue a lifelong ambition to become a writer, and has had many articles published in national magazines. He is a keen student of local history and enjoys visiting old churches in North Yorkshire and the Yorkshire Dales; his wife Shirley does most of the photography. With Shirley, he enjoys long distance travel, which has included four trips to Japan to see their son Jonathan who lives in Tokyo.

7. HIGH STREET AND QUARRY HILL

Jane Greenwood was born in Leeds and lived in Scholes until she was married in 1961. She now lives in Shadwell where she has been for the last thirty one years. She inherited an interest in the past from her fahter and through this gained a BA Honours degree from the Open University in 1995 concentrating mainly on European History. This gave her a love a travel in which she has been able to indulge these last two years. She has three sons a daughter all living locally. Her interests apart from social history are centred around the family and she has been busy researching her family tree. It was during this research her interests grew in the area around Quarry Hill. She says researching areas where her ancestors lived, and the times in which they lived brings people to life and they do not remain just names on a piece of paper. Family history is also a rich source of material for local history.

8. COLONEL HARDING AND THE BLACK PRINCE

William Scott was born and bred in Leeds, being educated at Roundhay School and with his wife Pat still lives in the City. Since leaving school (with a gap for National Service in Egypt) all his working career has been in the transport industry, including some 13 years as Operations Manager for British Waterways Board. Currently he is Managing Director of his own storage and ship handling company in Goole; he still deals occasionally with commercial barge transport. Apart from work his interests range from archaeology to local history and (as his two married daughters live in London and Cairo respectively) travel.

9. RELIGIOUS ROLES IN THE NINETEENTH CENTURY SOCIAL GROWTH OF BRAMLEY

Anthony Silson has always lived in Bramley, although he crossed the Pennines to study at Liverpool University. His interest in Bramley's history heightened as a result of redevelopment, and led him to write a book *Bramley: Half a Century of Change*. From St Peter's School Bramley he went to West Leeds High School where regrettably he had to choose between history and geography. He became a geographer and subsequently taught in Barnsley, Bradford and Leeds and has had several geographical articles published. His recent retirement has enabled him to devote more time to his historical interests. In 1996 he contributed a chapter to Railways *Around Whitby vol 2*, an area which interests him almost as much as Bramley.

10. A Year at St Anne's School Woodhouse Square 1952-3

Maureen Thorp was born in April 1940, just after the Battle of Britain and has been married to Gary for thirty eight years. They have two grown up sons and one grandson. Maureen is Leeds born and bred. She left school at the age of fifteen and worked in various jobs from blood donor attendent, super market shelf-filler, book keeper and administrator. Maureen sat 'O' level maths and english in the 1970s and after being made redundant in 1990 pursued a course of education which led to a BA (Hons) in Sociology and Media Studies in 1997. She has various interests from leisure, social and political and outdoor pursuits.

11. Zimmy's: A Glimpse of Factory Life in a Pre-War Clothing Factory

Isadore Pear was born in Leeds in 1920. He left school in 1934 at age of fourteen and worked in a clothing factory until he was conscripted in May 1940. He served six years in the West Yorshire Regiment and rose to the rank of Company Sergeant Major, Warrent Officer II. On being demobilized he went into business with his brother establishing the firm C & I Pear Ltd Clothing Manufacturers. He retired early at the age of fity-nine and enrolled at Park Lane College as a mature student taking A levels. He then went on to obtain an LLB(Hons) degree at Leeds Polytechnic. He is an active and prominent member of the Leeds Jewish Community and, although no longer involved, was a founder member of AJEX, the Association of Jewish Ex-Servicemen and Women in Leeds; an organisation which was formed initially to fight anti-semitism. He recently compiled the 120 years history of his synagogue the Beth Hamerdrash Hagadol, and is a regular contributor to its fortnightly broadsheet.

174

INDEX -PEOPLE

INDEX -GENERAL